FROM COLONIES TO COUNTRY
1735–1791

TEACHING GUIDE
FOR THE REVISED 3RD EDITION

Oxford University Press, Inc., publishes works that
further Oxford University's objective of excellence
in research, scholarship, and education.

Oxford   New York
Auckland   Cape Town   Dar es Salaam   Hong Kong   Karachi
Kuala Lumpur   Madrid   Melbourne   Mexico City   Nairobi
New Delhi   Shanghai   Taipei   Toronto

With offices in
Argentina   Austria   Brazil   Chile   Czech Republic   France   Greece
Guatemala   Hungary   Italy   Japan   Poland   Portugal   Singapore
South Korea   Switzerland   Thailand   Turkey   Ukraine   Vietnam

Writers: Joan Poole, Deborah Parks, Karen Edwards
Editors: Robert Weisser, Susan Moger
Editorial Consultant: Susan Buckley

Published by Oxford University Press, Inc.
198 Madison Avenue, New York, New York, 10016
www.oup.com

Oxford is a registered trademark of Oxford University Press

ISBN 978-0-19-518888-2

Project Editor: Matt Fisher
Project Director: Jacqueline A. Ball
Education Consultant: Diane L. Brooks, Ed.D.

Casper Grathwohl, Publisher

Printed in the United States
on acid-free paper

CONTENTS

NOTE FROM THE AUTHOR

Dear Teacher,

It is through story that people have traditionally passed on their ideas, their values, and their heritage. In recent years, however, we have come to think of stories as the property of the youngest of our children. How foolish of us. The rejection of story has made history seem dull. It has turned it into a litany of facts and dates. Stories make the past understandable (as well as enjoyable). Stories tell us who we are and where we've been. Without knowledge of our past, we can't make sense of the present.

As a former teacher, I knew of the need for a narrative history for young people, so I sat down and wrote one. (It took me seven years.) I was tired of seeing children struggle with arm-breaking, expensive books. I wanted my books to be inexpensive, light in weight, and user-friendly. Thanks to creative partnering by American Historical Publications and Oxford University Press, that's the way they are.

Called *A History of US,* mine is a set of 11 books. My hope is that they will help make American history—our story—a favorite subject again. It is important that it be so. As we prepare for the 21st century, we are becoming an increasingly diverse people. While we need to celebrate and enjoy that diversity, we also need to find solid ground to stand on together. Our history can provide that commonality. We are a nation built on ideas, on great documents, on individual achievement—and none of that is the property of any one group of us. Harriet Tubman, Abraham Lincoln, Emily Dickinson, Sequoya, and Duke Ellington belong to all of us—and so do our horse thieves, slave owners, and robber barons. We need to consider them all.

Now, to be specific, what do I intend these books to do in your classrooms? First of all, I want to help turn your students into avid readers. I want them to understand that nonfiction can be as exciting as fiction. (Besides, it is the kind of reading they'll meet most in the adult world.) I want to stretch their minds. I've written stories, but the stories are true stories. In nonfiction you grapple with the real world. I want to help children understand how fascinating that process can be.

I've tried to design books that I would have liked as a teacher—books that are flexible, easy-to-read, challenging, and idea-centered, that will lead children into energetic discussions. History can do that. It involves issues we still argue about. It gives us material with which to make judgments. It allows for comparisons. It hones the mind.

People all over this globe are dying—literally—because they want to live under a democracy. We've got the world's model and most of us don't understand or appreciate it. I want to help children learn about their country so they will be intelligent citizens. I want them to understand the heritage that they share with all the diverse people who are us—the citizens of the United States.

For some of your students, these books may be an introduction to history. What they actually remember will be up to you. Books can inspire and excite, but understanding big ideas and remembering details takes some reinforced learning. You'll find many suggestions for that in this Teaching Guide.

What you do with *A History of Us* and this Teaching Guide will depend, of course, on you and your class. You may have students read every chapter or only some chapters, many volumes or only a few. (But, naturally, I hope they'll read it all. Our history makes good reading.) I hope you'll use the books to teach reading and thinking skills as well as history and geography. We need to stop thinking of subjects as separate from each other. We talk about integrating the curriculum; we need to really do it. History, broadly, is the story of a culture—and that embraces art, music, science, mathematics, and literature. (You'll find some of all of those in these books.)

Reading *A History of Us* is easy; even young children seem to enjoy it. But some of the concepts in the books are not easy. They can be challenging to adults, which means that the volumes can be read on several levels. The idea is to get students excited by history and stretched mentally—at whatever their level of understanding. (Don't worry if every student doesn't understand every word. We adults don't expect that of our reading; we should allow for the same variety of comprehension among student readers.)

This Teaching Guide is filled with ideas meant to take the students back to the text to do a careful, searching read. It will also send them out to do research and writing and discovering on their own. The more you involve your students, the more they will understand and retain. Confucius, one of the worlds' great teachers, had this to say:

Tell me and I will forget. Show me and I will remember. Involve me and I will understand.

History is about discovering. It is a voyage that you and your students can embark on together. I wish you good sailing.

Joy Hakim with two of her favorite readers, her grandchildren, Natalie and Sam Johnson

THE HISTORY OF US PROGRAM

I. STUDENT EDITION

► By Joy Hakim, winner of James Michener Prize in Writing
► Engaging, friendly narrative
► A wide range of primary sources in every chapter
► Period illustrations and specially commissioned maps
► New atlas section customized for each book

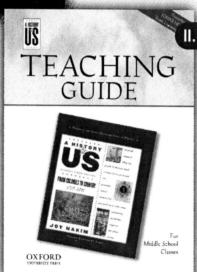

II. TEACHING GUIDE

► Standards-based instruction
► Wide range of activities and classroom approaches
► Strategies for universal access and improving literacy (ELL, struggling readers, advanced learners)
► Multiple assessment tools

III. STUDENT STUDY GUIDE

► Exercises correlated to Student Edition and Teaching Guide
► Portfolio approach
► Activities for every level of learning
► Literacy through reading and writing
► Completely new for 2005

SOURCEBOOK AND INDEX

► Broad selection of primary sources in each subject area
► Ideal resource for in-class exercises and unit projects

Each Teaching Guide is organized into Parts. Each Part includes Chapter Lessons, a Team Learning Project from Johns Hopkins University, Check-up Tests, and other assessments and activities

PARTS
Unify chapter lessons with themes and projects.

INTRODUCTION
► Lists standards addressed in each chapter
► Gives objectives and big ideas and suggests projects and lessons to set context for the chapters

SUMMARY
► Gives assessment ideas and debate, ethics, and interdisciplinary project ideas

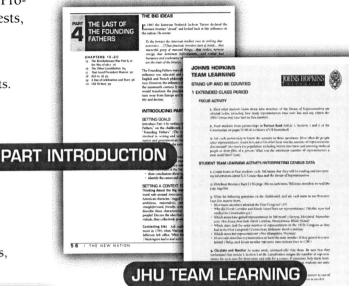

PART INTRODUCTION

JHU TEAM LEARNING

JHU TEAM LEARNING
► Each Part contains a cooperative learning project developed by the Talent Development Middle School Program at Johns Hopkins University specifically for *A History of US.*

CHAPTER LESSONS
► Correlated to the new Student Study Guide
► Ideas for enrichment, discussion, writing, vocabulary, and projects

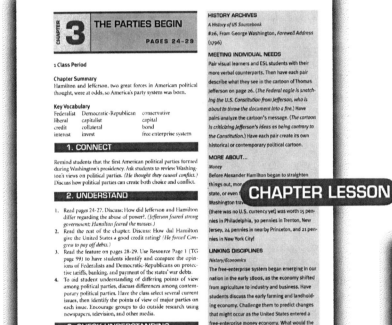

CHAPTER LESSON

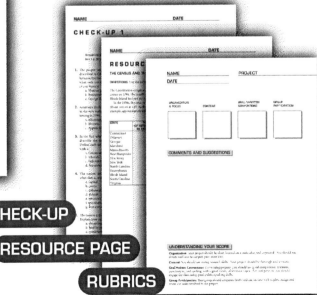

RUBRICS, CHECK-UPS, AND RESOURCE PAGES
► Reproduce and hand out for assessment and activities

CHECK-UP

RESOURCE PAGE

RUBRICS

PLANNING LESSONS USING TEACHING AND STUDENT STUDY GUIDES

SET A CONTEXT FOR READING

The books in *A History of US* are written so that a student can read them from cover to cover. You can strengthen students' connection to major themes through introductory lessons or projects. These lessons can be found in the introduction to the Teaching Guide and the opening pages for each Part.

Some students, especially developing readers or those learning English as a second language, may need extra help building background knowledge before reading the text. For these students, exercises in the Teaching and Student Study Guides help to set a context for reading. Look for **Connect** (in the Teaching Guide) and **Access** (in the Student Study Guide) sections. Also, refer to the Improving Literacy section (pages 20–25) for general strategies from an expert.

CREATE A FLEXIBLE CLASSROOM PLAN USING THE STUDENT STUDY GUIDE AND TEACHING GUIDE

The ancillary materials for *A History of US* have been developed for multiple teaching strategies, depending on the particular needs and abilities of your students. Choose an approach that works best for your students. Here are a few options:

▶ **Assign Student Study Guide activities as best suits your class needs**
The Student Study Guide activities are designed to reinforce and clarify content. They were created for students to complete with a minimum of explanation or supervision. The Student Study Guide can be used as homework or in class. The activities can be assigned concurrently with the reading, to help comprehend the material and come to class ready for in-depth discussion of the reading, or as a follow-up to the reading.

▶ **Use Teaching Guide activities to build and enrich comprehension**
The activities from the **Understand** section of each Chapter Lesson, as well as the sidebars, are meant to foster a dynamic, active, vocal classroom. They center on participatory small group and partner projects and focused individual work.

▶ **Use group projects to broaden understanding**
Other suggestions for group projects are found throughout the Teaching Guide, in Part Openers, Part Summaries, and Chapter Lessons. These activities cover a variety of content standard-related topics.

Also, developed specially for *A History of US* are the Johns Hopkins Team Learning Activities, which correlate to Part-wide themes and use cooperative learning models developed by Johns Hopkins University's Talent Development Middle School Program. (For more on these activities and how to use them, see page 21.) Also published by Oxford University Press, a complete curriculum, based on Team Learning Activities for *A History of US* is available. For more information, log on to *www.oup.com*.

Whether projects and assignments are geared toward solidifying understanding of the text or enriching connections with other disciplines is up to you.

▶ **Assign individual work**
Many exercises from the Teaching Guide **Check Understanding** section can be used for individual homework assignments. Student Study Guide pages can be assigned for homework as well.

▶ **Encourage students to create history journals for a portfolio approach**
Student Study Guide pages can be removed from the book and kept in a binder with writing assignments, artwork, and notes from projects as an individual portfolio. This approach creates a history journal, which has many benefits. It can be worked on at home and brought into class for assessment or sharing. It is a student's very own journal, where personal creativity can find an outlet. It also keeps all work organized and in order. Both the Teaching Guide and Student Study Guide contain a variety of analytical and creative writing projects that can be addressed in the history journal.

▶ **Assess however and whenever you need to**
This Teaching Guide contains the following assessment tools: cumulative, synthesis-based project ideas at the end of each Part, wrap-up tests, and scoring rubrics.

RUBRICS
At the back of this Teaching Guide you will find four reproducible rubric pages.

1. The Scoring Rubric page explains the evaluation categories. You may wish to go over and discuss each of these categories and points with your students.

2. A shortened handout version of the Scoring Rubric page has been included, with explanations of the categories and room for comments.

3. A student self-scoring rubric has been included. Use it to prompt your students to describe and evaluate both their work and participation in group projects.

4. A library/media center research log has also been included. Use this rubric as an aid to student research. It will help them plan and brainstorm research methods, record results, and evaluate their sources.

ASSESSMENT OPPORTUNITIES
Part Summaries were written specifically to give assessment ideas. They do this in two ways:

1. They refer to Part Check-Ups—reproducible tests at the back of the Teaching Guide that combine multiple choice, short answer, and an essay question to present a comprehensive assessment that covers the chapters in each Part.

2. They contains additional essay questions for alternate assessment as well as numerous project ideas. Projects can be assessed using the scoring rubrics at the back of the Teaching Guide.

ANSWER KEYS
An answer key at the back of the Teaching Guide contains answers for Part Check-Ups, Resource Pages, and Student Study Guide activities.

The Student Study Guide complements the activities in the Teaching Guide with exercises that build a context for the reading and strengthen analysis skills. Many activities encourage informal small group or family participation. In addition, the following features make it an effective teaching tool:

FLEXIBILITY

You can use the Study Guide in the classroom, with individuals or small groups, or send it home for homework. You can distribute the entire guide to students; however, the pages are perforated so you can remove and distribute only the pertinent lessons.

A page on reports and special projects in the front of the Study Guide directs students to the "More Books to Read" resource in the student edition. This feature gives students general guidance on doing research and devising independent study projects of their own.

FACSIMILE SPREAD

The Study Guide begins with a facsimile spread from the Student Edition. This spread gives reading strategies and highlights key features: captions, primary sources, sidebars, headings, etymologies. The spread supplies the contextualization students need to fully understand the material.

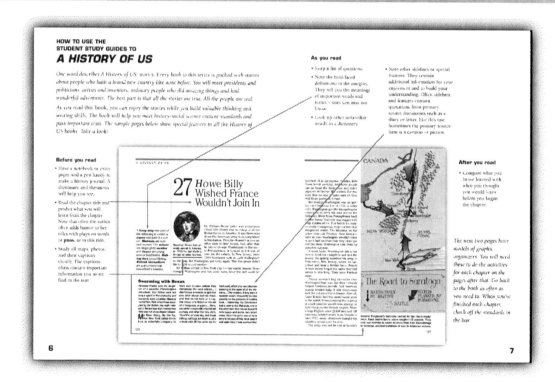

PORTFOLIO APPROACH

The Study Guide pages are three-hole-punched so they can be integrated with notebook paper in a looseleaf binder. This history journal or portfolio can become both a record of content mastery and an outlet for each student's unique creative expression. Responding to prompts, students can write poetry or songs, plays and character sketches, create storyboards or cartoons, or construct multi-layered timelines.

The portfolio approach gives students unlimited opportunities for practice in areas that need strengthening. And the Study Guide pages in the portfolio make a valuable assessment tool for you. It is an ongoing record of performance that can be reviewed and graded periodically.

GRAPHIC ORGANIZERS

This feature contains reduced models of seven graphic organizers referenced frequently in the guide. Using these devices will help students organize the material so it is more accessible. (Full-size reproducibles of each graphic organizer are provided at the back of this Teaching Guide.) These graphic organizers include: outline, main idea map, K-W-L chart (What I Know, What I Want to Know, What I Learned), Venn diagram, timeline, sequence of events chart, and t-chart.

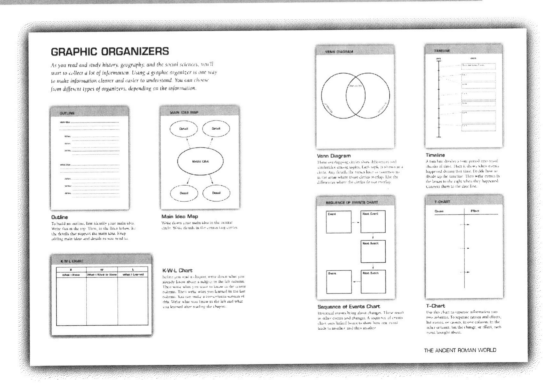

Each chapter lesson is designed to draw students into the subject matter. Recurring features and exercises challenge their knowledge and allow them to practice valuable analysis skills. Activities in the Teaching Guide and Student Study Guide complement but do not duplicate each other. Together they offer a wide range of class work, group projects, and opportunities for further study and assessment that can be tailored to all ability levels.

CHAPTER SUMMARY
briefly reviews big ideas from the chapter.

ACCESS
makes content accessible to students of all levels by incorporating graphic organizers into note taking.

WRITING
gives students writing suggestions drawn from the material. A writing assignment may stem from a vocabulary word, a historical event, a person, or a reading of a primary source. The assignment can take any number of forms: newspaper article, letter, short essay, a scene with dialogue, a diary entry.

CHAPTER 2

ABOUT BEING A PRESIDENT

SUMMARY *George Washington chose advisers to help him run the country.*

ACCESS

Have you ever tried to do a really hard job by yourself? Hard jobs are usually easier when you get people to help. President Washington could not run the country by himself. He needed advisers to assist him. Copy the main idea map from page 8 into your history journal. In the largest circle, put Washington's name. In each of the smaller circles, write the name of one of the people who helped Washington govern the nation. Below each name, write the job that the person had.

WORD BANK   precedent   executive   legislative   judicial   cabinet   dictatorship

Choose words from the word bank to complete the sentences. One word is not used at all.

1. The _____ branch includes the nation's courts.

2. A government that is run by an all-powerful leader is called a _____.

3. The president is the head of the _____ branch.

4. Washington chose Henry Knox to serve in his _____.

5. Congress is also called the _____ branch.

WORD PLAY

In the dictionary, look up the word you did not use. Write a sentence using that word.

_____

WITH A PARENT OR PARTNER

The United States has a three-branch government. Write the name of each branch at the top of a piece of paper. Below each name, write five words that relate to that particular branch of government. Ask a parent or partner to do the same. Then read your lists to each other.

WORKING WITH PRIMARY SOURCES

In 1792 Dr. Benjamin Rush wrote this about a hot air balloon flight by Jean-Pierre François Blanchard:

> For some time days past the conversation in our city has turned wholly upon Mr. Blanchard's late Aerial Voyage. It was truly a sublime sight. Every faculty of the mind was seized, expanded and captivated by it, 40,000 people concentrating their eyes and thoughts at the same instant, upon the same object, and all deriving nearly the same degree of pleasure from it.

1. How did Benjamin Rush feel about Blanchard's flight?

2. How did the people of Philadelphia feel about Blanchard's flight?

WRITING

Imagine that you are in Philadelphia watching Blanchard's flight. In your history journal, write a letter to a friend describing the event in your own words.

12   CHAPTER 2

CHAPTER 3

THE PARTIES BEGIN

SUMMARY *Alexander Hamilton and Thomas Jefferson had different ideas about what was best for the country. Their disagreements led to America's first party system.*

ACCESS

What is a political party? How many political parties can you think of? When George Washington took office, the United States did not have any political parties. He thought they caused conflict. Copy the main idea map from page 8 into your history journal. In the largest circle, put *Hamilton and Jefferson's Disagreements.* As you read the chapter, write an issue they disagreed about in each of the smaller circles.

WORD BANK

> Federalist   liberal   credit   interest   Democratic-Republican   capitalist   collateral   invest   conservative   capital   bond   free enterprise system

Choose words from the word bank to complete the sentences. One word is not used at all.

1. Thomas Jefferson was the leader of the _____ party.

2. If you borrow money, you must pay _____.

3. A capitalist system is sometimes called a _____.

4. A _____ favors civil liberties, democratic reforms and the use of governmental power to promote social progress.

5. The _____ party consisted of Alexander Hamilton's supporters.

6. When people get a loan, sometimes they must provide _____.

7. A _____ is a written promise to pay back a loan.

8. Many farmers and solders decided to _____ in the new U.S. government.

9. A _____ is someone who is reluctant to make changes.

10. Another word for borrowing power is _____.

11. _____ is money, or any goods or assets that can be turned into money.

WORD PLAY

Identify two of the above terms that have similar meanings. Next identify two of the above terms that have opposite meanings. Write your answers below.

_____

CRITICAL THINKING COMPARE AND CONTRAST

The phrases below describe Alexander Hamilton and Thomas Jefferson. In your history journal, copy the Venn Diagram on page 9. Write *Hamilton* above one circle and *Jefferson* above the other circle. The phrases that apply to only one person go in that person's circle. The phrases that apply to both go in the area where the two circles connect.

wanted a free education amendment	had faith in ordinary people	fought for freedom of the press
concerned about balancing liberty and power	feared the masses	encouraged business and industry
wanted the government to pay off its debt	headed a major political party	
wanted aristocratic leaders to govern	feared a powerful government	

WORKING WITH PRIMARY SOURCES

Stephen Vincent Benét wrote a poem about one of the Founding Fathers.

He could handle the Nation's dollars	And scratch like a wildcat, too.
With a magic that's known to few,	And he yoked the States together
He could talk with the wits and scholars	With a yoke that is strong and stout.

Who is the subject of the poem? Which lines reveal the person's identity? Circle your answers in the poem.

THE NEW NATION   **13**

WORD BANK
reinforces key vocabulary from the student book and Teaching Guide.

CRITICAL THINKING
exercises draw on such thinking skills as establishing cause and effect, making inferences, drawing conclusions, determining sequence of events, comparing and contrasting, identifying main ideas and details, and other analytical process.

WORKING WITH PRIMARY SOURCES
invites students to read primary sources closely. Exercises include answering comprehension questions, evaluating point of view, and writing.

Strategic Methods for Content Learning

READING HISTORY

A PRACTICAL GUIDE TO IMPROVING LITERACY

JANET ALLEN

with Christine Landaker

Enhancing reading skills and learning history are inextricably linked. Students for whom reading is a challenge have difficulty immersing themselves in books and in historical narratives. With these students, improving literacy becomes crucial for teaching history.

Especially with struggling readers and English-language learners, comprehending the text is the first (and often most difficult) step toward engaging the story. *Reading History: A Practical Guide to Improving Literacy*, by Dr. Janet Allen, was written specifically to address teaching history to these students. *Reading History* is a book of instructional strategies for "building meaningful background knowledge that will support reading, writing, and research."

The instructional strategies in *Reading History* are modular components that can be understood with a minimum of instruction and can be applied easily as pre- and post-reading and writing activities. The Wordstorming and List-Group-Label exercises below are two examples of the simple and effective activities that can be the difference between giving information and building background that helps to improve literacy.

Dr. Allen and colleague Christine Landaker used *A History of US* to help create and illustrate the activities in *Reading History*, and examples from *A History of US* appear throughout the book, dovetailing the two books into a single, comprehensive, and successful literacy-based History curriculum.

From Reading History

WORDSTORMING

1. Ask students to write down all the words they can think of related to a given word (concept, theme, target word).

2. When students have exhausted their contributions, help them add to their individual lists by giving some specific directions.
   Can you think of words that describe someone without _____?
   Can you think of words that would show what someone might see, hear, feel, touch, smell in a situation filled with _____?

3. Ask students to group and label their words.

4. Add any words you think should be included and ask students to put them in the right group.

LIST-GROUP-LABEL

1. List all of the words you can think of related to _____ (major concept of text).

2. Group words that you have listed by words that have something in common.

3. Once words are grouped, decide on a label for each group.

USING THE JOHNS HOPKINS TEAM LEARNING ACTIVITIES

JOHNS HOPKINS
U N I V E R S I T Y

The Talent Development Middle School Program at Johns Hopkins University is a project of the Center for the Social Organization of Schools (CSOS). *A History of US* is the core of the American history curriculum in this whole-school reform effort. Oxford University Press proudly includes in this Teaching Guide selected lessons developed by Susan Dangel and Maria Gariott at the Talent Development Middle School Program.

You will find one Johns Hopkins Team Learning Activity at the end of each Part in this Teaching Guide. Keyed to appropriate chapters, the Team Learning Activity provides an opportunity to use cooperative learning models based on *A History of US*.

Each Activity begins with a Focus Activity that introduces the lesson, engages students, and draws on students' prior knowledge.

The heart of the lesson is a Team Learning Activity. In teams, students investigate lesson content, solve problems, use information for a purpose, and apply the tools of the historian.

Within the Student Team Learning Activity, the following techniques and strategies may be employed:

▶ Brainstorming: Students generate as many ideas as possible within a set time, before discussing and evaluating them.

▶ Roundtable: A brainstorming technique in which each team member contributes ideas on one sheet of paper and passes it to the next student. In Simultaneous Roundtable, more than one sheet is passed at the same time.

▶ Round Robin: An oral form of brainstorming in which one team member at a time states an idea.

▶ Think-Pair-Share: Students think about content or consider a question, then share their responses with a partner. In Think-Team-Share, students think through the prompt on their own and then share as a team.

▶ Partner Read: Students share a reading assignment with a partner.

▶ Timed Telling: A student or team is given a fixed time to share information, opinions, or results with the class.

▶ Team Investigation: Working in teams, students search and analyze the text, primary source materials, or other resource materials; draw conclusions; and make connections.

▶ Jigsaw: Within each team, students select or are assigned specific questions or subjects on which to become experts. Experts meet and investigate in Expert Teams, then regroup in their original teams to report out their findings.

▶ Numbered Heads: Each team member is assigned a number—1, 2, 3, and so on. Team members work together on the team learning activity. The teacher selects one number and asks the person with that number in each team to report the team response.

PROVIDING ACCESS

The books in this series are written in a lively, narrative style to inspire a love of reading. English language learners and struggling readers are given special consideration within the program's exercises and activities. And students who love to read and learn will also benefit from the program's rich and varied material. Following are expert strategies to make sure each and every student gets the most out of the subjects you will teach through *A History of US*.

ADVANCED LEARNERS

Every classroom has students who finish the required assignments and then want additional challenges. Fortunately, the very nature of history and social science offers a wide range of opportunities for students to explore topics in greater depth. Encourage them to come up with their own ideas for an additional assignment. Determine the final product, its presentation, and a timeline for completion.

Research

Students can develop in-depth understanding through seeking information, exploring ideas, asking and answering questions, making judgments, considering points of view, and evaluating actions and events. They will need access to a wide range of resource materials: the Internet, maps, encyclopedias, trade books, magazines, dictionaries, artifacts, newspapers, museum catalogues, brochures, and the library. See the "More Books to Read" section at the end of the Student Edition for good jumping-off points.

Projects

You can encourage students to capitalize on their strengths as learners (visual, verbal, kinesthetic, or musical) or to try a new way of responding. Students can prepare a debate or write a persuasive paper, play, skit, poem, song, dance, game, puzzle, or biography. They can create an alphabet book on the topic, film a video, do a book talk, or illustrate a book. They can render charts, graphs, or other visual representations. Allow for creativity and support students' thinking.

ENGLISH LANGUAGE LEARNERS

For English learners to achieve academic success, the instructional considerations for teachers include two mandates:

- ▶ Help them attain grade level, content area knowledge, and academic language.
- ▶ Provide for the development of English language proficiency.

To accomplish these goals, you should plan lessons that reflect the student's level of English proficiency. Students progress through five developmental levels as they increase in language proficiency:

- ▶ Beginning and Early Intermediate (grade level material will be mostly incomprehensible, students need a great deal of teacher support)
- ▶ Intermediate (grade level work will be a challenge)
- ▶ Early Advanced and Advanced (close to grade level reading and writing, students continue to need support)

Tap Prior Knowledge

What students know about the topic will help determine your next steps for instruction. Using K-W-L charts, brainstorming, and making lists are ways to find out what they know. English learners bring a rich cultural diversity into the classroom. By sharing what they know, students can connect their knowledge and experiences to the course.

Set the Context

Use different tools to make new information understandable. These can be images, artifacts, maps, timelines, illustrations, charts, videos, or graphic organizers. Techniques such as role-playing and storyboarding can also be helpful. Speak in shorter sentences, with careful enunciation, expanded explanations, repetitions, and paraphrasing. Use fewer idiomatic expressions.

Show—Don't Just Tell

English learners often get lost as they listen to directions, explanations, lectures, and discussions. By showing students what is expected, you can help them participate more fully in classroom activities. Students need to be shown how to use the graphic organizers in the student study guide, as well as other blackline masters for note-taking and practice. An overhead transparency with whole or small groups is also effective.

Use the Text

Because of unfamiliar words, students will need help with understanding. Teach them to preview the chapter using text features (headings, bold print, sidebars, italics). See the suggestions in the facsimile of the Student Edition, shown on pages 6–7 of the Student Study Guide. Show students organizing structures such as cause and effect or comparing and contrasting. Have students read to each other in pairs. Help them create word banks, charts, and graphic organizers. Discuss the main idea after reading.

Check for Understanding

Rather than simply ask students if they understand, stop frequently and ask them to paraphrase or expand on what you just said. Such techniques will give you a much clearer assessment of their understanding.

Provide for Interaction

As students interact with the information and speak their thoughts, their content knowledge and academic language skills improve. Increase interaction in the classroom through cooperative learning, small group work, and partner share. By working and talking with others, students can practice asking and answering questions.

Use Appropriate Assessment

When modifying the instruction, you will also need to modify the assessment. Multiple choice, true and false, and other criterion reference tests are suitable, but consider changing test format and structure. English learners are constantly improving their language proficiency in their oral and written responses, but they are often grammatically incorrect. Remember to be thoughtful and fair about giving students credit for their content knowledge and use of academic language, even if their English isn't perfect.

STRUGGLING READERS

Some students struggle to understand the information presented in a textbook. The following strategies for content-area reading can help students improve their ability to make comparisons, sequence events, determine importance, summarize, evaluate, synthesize, analyze, and solve problems.

Build Knowledge of Genre

Both fiction and narrative nonfiction genres are incorporated into *A History of US*. This combination of genres makes the text interesting and engaging. But teachers must be sure students can identify and use the organizational structures of both genres.

The textbook has a wealth of the text features of nonfiction: bold and italic print, sidebars, headings and subheadings, labels, captions, and "signal words" such as first, next, and finally. Teaching these organizational structures and text features is essential for struggling readers.

Fiction

Each chapter is a story

Setting: historical time and place

Characters: historical figures

Plot: problems, roadblocks, and resolutions

Non-Fiction

Content: historical information

Organizational structure: cause/effect, sequence of events, problem/solution

Other features: maps, timelines, sidebars, photographs, primary sources

Build Background

Having background information about a topic makes reading about it so much easier. When students lack background information, teachers can preteach or "front load" concepts and vocabulary, using a variety of instructional techniques. Conduct a "chapter or bookwalk," looking at titles, headings, and other text features to develop a big picture of the content. Focus in new vocabulary words during the "walk" and create a word bank with illustrations for future reference. Read aloud key passages and discuss the meaning. Focus on the timeline and maps to help students develop a sense of time and place. Show a video, go to a website, and have trade books and magazines on the topic available for student exploration.

Comprehension Strategies

While reading, successful readers are predicting, making connections, monitoring, visualizing, questioning, inferring, and summarizing. Struggling readers have a harder time with these "in the head" processes. The following strategies will help these students construct meaning from the text until they are able to do it on their own.

Predict

Before reading, conduct a picture and text feature "tour" of the chapter to make predictions. Ask students if they remember if this has ever happened before, to predict what might happen this time.

Make Connections

Help students relate content to their background (text to text, text to self, and text to the world).

Monitor And Confirm

Encourage students to stop reading when they come across an unknown word, phrase, or concept. In their notebooks, have them make a note of text they don't understand and ask for clarification or figure it out. While this activity slows down reading at first, it is effective in improving skills over time.

Visualize

Students benefit from imagining the events described in a story. Sketching scenes, story-boarding, role-playing, and looking for sensory details all help students with this strategy.

Infer

Help students look beyond the literal meaning of a text to understand deeper meanings. Graphic organizers and discussions provide opportunities to broaden their understanding. Looking closely at the "why" of historical events helps students infer.

Question And Discuss

Have students jot down their questions as they read, and then share them during discussions. Or have students come up with the type of questions they think a teacher would ask. Over time students will develop more complex inferential questions, which lead to group discussions. Questioning and discussing also helps students see ideas from multiple perspectives and draw conclusions, both critical skills for understanding history.

Determine Importance

Teach students how to decide what is most important from all the facts and details in nonfiction. After reading for an overall understanding, they can go back to highlight important ideas, words, and phrases. Clues for determining importance include bold or italic print, signal words, and other text features. A graphic organizer such as a main idea map also helps.

Teach and Practice Decoding Strategies

Rather than simply defining an unfamiliar word, teach struggling readers decoding strategies: have them look at the prefix, suffix, and root to help figure out the new word, look for words they know within the word, use the context for clues, and read further or reread.

— Cheryl A. Caldera, M.A.
Literacy Coach

TEACHING STRATEGIES FOR
FROM COLONIES TO COUNTRY

INTRODUCING BOOK THREE

HISTORICAL OVERVIEW

When in the Course of human events it becomes necessary for one people to dissolve the political bands which have connected them with another, and to assume among the Powers of the earth the separate and equal station to which the Laws of Nature and of Nature's God entitle them, a decent respect to the opinions of mankind requires that they should declare the causes which impel them to the separation.

With these words, Thomas Jefferson formally announced the severing of ties that stretched back to Jamestown, Plymouth, and Massachusetts Bay. Approved on July 4, 1776, the Declaration of Independence told the world that Americans intended to build a new nation—a nation that would join the world community on an equal footing with other nations.

Like most conflicts, the Revolution that followed the Declaration did not burst spontaneously on the world scene. Tensions with the home country existed throughout much of the colonial period. A century earlier, for example, rebels led by Nathaniel Bacon tried to chase the royal governor out of Jamestown. A year later, in 1677, North Carolinians rebelled against English taxes. When royal officials tried to clamp down on New England in the 1680s, they found that the Puritans could be just as rebellious as their southern neighbors.

None of these earlier conflicts, however, lasted for long. Nor were they widespread. More important, most conflicts were fought to redefine relationships with the home country, not to end them. Colonists considered themselves English citizens with the rights and liberties guaranteed by English law and custom. That's what the trial of John Peter Zenger was all about—defending freedom of speech and press against the arbitrary abuse of royal power.

Starting in the 1750s and 1760s, colonists' attitudes toward the home country started to change. They began to question policies that formed the very foundation of colonialism. As an imperial power, Britain claimed the right to govern the colonies for the benefit of the home country. When the English government refused to treat them as equals, colonists began to take a long hard look at their political status within the empire. As John Adams later remarked, "The Revolution was affected before the war commenced."

Adams rooted the start of the Revolution in the French and Indian War. So do many historians. Britain's overwhelming victory in the war forever changed the balance of power in North America. Native Americans, for example, could no longer play the French and British against each other. As a result, they lost a valuable negotiating tool. On the other hand, the war robbed Britain of powerful diplomatic leverage against the colonists. With France swept from the continent, the colonists had little need for British protection against a foreign enemy.

The British victory in 1763 changed relations between the colonies and home country in other ways as well. Burdened with heavy debts from the war, Great Britain passed a series of laws and taxes in an effort to force colonists to share in the costs of empire. It also tried to avoid further wars by sealing off the frontier with the Proclamation of 1763. The new tax and land poli-

Boston Tea Party

Thomas Paine's *Common Sense*

FROM TOP TO BOTTOM: Patriots attack a Loyalist; First draft of the Declaration of Independence; Washington at Valley Forge; Siege of Yorktown

Patriots attack a Loyalist

First draft of the Declaration of Independence

cies exposed differences between the political thinking of the British and colonists.

In the 1760s, colonists formed coalitions to resist British efforts to tighten control of the colonial assemblies. At first, few considered independence. However, British refusal to compromise fueled colonial militancy. Finally, in 1775, tempers snapped at Lexington and Concord. The blood spilled that day began one of the only two wars ever fought on United States soil. (The other was the Civil War.)

With Patriots and Redcoats scuffling in New England, the Continental Congress struggled to define the conflict. In July 1776, delegates named it a political revolution for independence. Winning for the British meant crushing the rebels. For the colonists, on the other hand, winning meant that they only to endure and avoid capture.

Jefferson wrote the Declaration of Independence to win support for the Patriot cause both at home and abroad. Its lofty ideals, however, brought far-reaching changes to America. At the core of these changes lay a commitment to republicanism, or the idea that government should rest solely on the consent of the people. When the war ended, the new nation had to turn that commitment into reality. Remarked Connecticut poet Joel Barlow in 1781:

The Revolution is but half completed. Independence and government were the two objects contended for and but one is obtained.

To obtain the "second object," Americans entered into a remarkable period of constitution writing, first at the state level and then at the national level. The final product, the Constitution of the United States, gave the world its first working blueprint for a federal republic. It took ideals from English laws and the Enlightenment and put them into practice. It also introduced some uniquely American principles of government, such as the separation of church and state.

Today the Constitution is the world's oldest working written plan of government. The road leading to creation of this document forms the story of Book Three.

ABOVE: Washington at Valley Forge; LEFT: Siege of Yorktown

INTRODUCING THE BIG IDEAS

Conflict and **change** are the two Big Ideas in *From Colonies to Country*. They provide the conceptual framework that holds together the 42 chapters and hundreds of stories in this volume of *A History of US*.

Introducing your students to these concepts at the beginning will help them put together the pieces of the puzzle to make sense of the past. One starting point would be to write on the chalkboard the title of this book—*From Colonies to Country*—followed by the words *conflict* and *change*. Open a discussion of conflict and change and how they can be related. Have students consider Book Three's title and then predict what major change will be described in the book and how conflict might have been involved in that change. (The discussion may be speculative to quite specific, depending on students' prior historical knowledge.) You may want to make an analogy to changes and consequent conflict in students' own lives as they grow up and become more independent.

FOCUSING ON LITERACY

SETTING THE CONTEXT
Undoubtedly, your students are coming to Book Three after a study of the colonial period. Set the context for reading this volume by writing on the chalkboard or reading aloud the title of the seven parts of Book Three. (See TG page 3.)

To set the stage for Book Three, have students read the Preface on pages 9-12. You might request several "storytellers" to read the material aloud. After discussing the ideas in the Preface, challenge students to write letters in which they describe to a friend their journey back in time. In the closing paragraphs of the letter, students should describe the changes that they see ahead.

CHARTING CAUSE AND EFFECT
The events in Book Three lend themselves to an analysis of cause and effect that will help students organize their thoughts and understanding. Set up large sheets of paper on which students can create ongoing and changing diagrams showing the causes and effects of significant events such as the French and Indian War or the Stamp Act.

READING FURTHER
Book Three's period of American history—pre- through post-American Revolution—is covered in widely available books for young readers and heavily illustrated histories for all ages. Encourage students to visit their school and community libraries to find books and bring them in to create a temporary classroom library on this period. For extra credit, have students join in groups to use these books to create different units for the class. For example, one group might create a "Heroes of the Time" collected biography. Another might create a bulletin board display illustrating "Steps Toward Liberty." Other topics for development might include "David (American colonies) vs. Goliath (Great Britain)," "Great Military Moments," and "Creating a Brand New Government."

INTRODUCING THE BOOK WITH PROJECTS AND ACTIVITIES

USING THE RUBRICS

To assess these writing assignments, group projects, and activities, scoring rubrics have been provided at the back to this Teaching Guide. Be sure to explain the rubrics to your students.

REPRODUCIBLE MAPS

At the back of both this guide and Student Study Guide are reproducible maps for geography activities for From Colonies to Country. _The activities in the Teaching Guide and Student Study Guide will refer to the correct reproducible map by its title. Feel free to duplicate these maps for additional activities._

ONGOING PROJECTS

The following activities bridge the seven parts in _From Colonies to Country._

USING TIME LINES

As author Joy Hakim advises (see Note from the Author on this page), a sense of chronology is what matters for students. Various kinds of time lines are invaluable aids in building this understanding of historical sequence.

A class time line of American history, started at the beginning of the year, will help students place each segment of this study in sequence. You and your class can create such a time line with long sheets of butcher paper. Connected sheets of computer paper or even clothesline (see Note from the Author)—also work well.

Students can also use the same techniques to create smaller class and personal time lines focusing on the main block of time covered in Book Three. Let students calculate as a group or individually how to divide up the time line. You may want to create one for 1700-1800 or a more specific time line for 1735-1795.

Suggest that students allow enough room for describing and/or illustrating events on the time line. As students work their way through the various chapters in the book, they should update and extend the time line.

Assessment/Sequencing When students have completed the class or individual time lines, have them design charts entitled _The Road to Self-Government._ Have students list items from the time line that were important milestones on the way to our federal republic (for example, Albany Plan of Union, Stamp Act Congress, Committees of Correspondence, First and Second Continental Congresses, Declaration of Independence, Articles of Confederation, state constitutions, Constitutional Convention, ratification of the Constitution). Call on students to offer their milestones to create a sequence on the chalkboard. As each is identified, ask students to discuss how it contributed to eventual self-government.

USING MAPS

Students should trace the changes and conflicts in Book Three on a large classroom map as well as on individual maps. Encourage students to locate the actions they are reading about on a topographical map, to see what kind of terrain is involved and thus how geographical features might affect the actions.

Colonial Era Map Have students trace important events from the colonial period on a Colonial Era wall or reproducible map. Activities for chapters 2-19 will suggest ongoing additions to the Colonial Era map under the heading Geography Connections: Colonial Era Map Activity. To help reinforce map reading skills, you may wish to have students locate important places by the map coordinates provided or by directions from the nearest major town/settlement, or by referring to maps from the book. If using the reproducible maps for this activity, use the Eastern US Relief map. Have students keep the map in their history journals.

Revolutionary War Room Map Have students create a "war room" map tracing the battles and events of the Revolutionary war on a wall or reproducible map. Activities for chapters 22-31 will suggest ongoing additions to the Revolutionary War Room map under the heading Geography Connections: War Room map Activity. To help reinforce map reading skills, you may wish to have students locate important places by the map coordinates provided or by directions from the nearest major town/settlement, or by referring to maps from the book. Have students label British and American troop movements and battle victories. If using the reproducible maps for this activity, use the Revolutionary War map. Have students keep the map in their history journals.

WRITING HISTORY

Help students make American history their own by encouraging them to retell and add to the stories in *A History of US.* One way to accomplish this is to ask students to set up a separate section in their notebooks or three-ring binders in which they write their own history books.

When you finish each chapter, give students time to write their own account of the events. (Some students may want to illustrate their histories, too.) Encourage them to do additional research, to look more deeply into topics that interest them. (Point out that Joy Hakim often suggests ideas for further investigation right in the book.) From time to time, ask volunteers to share their histories with the class.

Assessment/Editing Historical Writing When students have finished compiling their own history books for Book Three, have them exchange these books with other students. Challenge students to pick one or two chapters in their classmate's book for editing. On a separate sheet of paper, students can list suggestions for needed clarifications or other improvements. They should also note well-written or especially interesting selections. Student editors should meet with "authors" to discuss the changes. After "authors" have revised their work, call on volunteers to read their revised history chapters aloud. Encourage them to note the tips that helped improve their writing.

TEACHING HISTORY

As a cooperative learning activity, you can assign teams of students to teach portions of the book. Remind students that the best teaching and learning occurs when everyone is involved. Students should think beyond lectures. Encourage them to enrich instruction with pictures, poems, art, and so on. The "teachers" should also devise short homework assignments or in-class activities. At the end of the lesson, they should submit several questions to the class that ask what they liked and did not like about the teaching of the lesson. What kinds of materials did they find enriching and not so enriching? Which teaching techniques worked well, and which did not?

Assessment/Self-Analysis Encourage "teachers" to use their own reactions to their teaching and the results of their poll of the class to evaluate their experience for themselves. What did they think worked best for them? Why? What would they want to improve? How? What suggestions might they make for teaching *A History of US*?

NOTE FROM THE AUTHOR
I like to ask students to write their own tests. They have to think to do that. Then I have them answer their own questions and someone else's as well.

PART 1

THE SEEDS OF CONFLICT

CHAPTERS 1–6

THE BIG IDEAS

In 1818, John Adams, one of the architects of American independence, reflected on the causes of the Revolution:

The Revolution was affected before the war commenced. The Revolution was in the hearts and minds of the people....This radical change in principles, opinions, and sentiments of the people was the real American Revolution.

Long before shots rang out at Lexington, the forces of conflict and change had begun to alter the hearts and minds of Americans. How these forces were set in motion is the subject of Part 1.

INTRODUCING PART 1

SETTING GOALS

Introduce Part 1 by writing its title on the chalkboard. Ask the class what seeds are and what they do. *(Seeds may be so small that you can't notice them. From underground seeds, large plants—even huge trees—may grow.)* Discuss with students what "seeds" might grow into conflict.

To set goals for Part 1, tell students that they will
• understand the conflict between colonial powers in North America.
• explain how the French and Indian War changed the political landscape of North America.
• identify and describe the sources of the conflict that arose between England and its American colonies.
• identify the roles of the key figures in this conflict.

SETTING A CONTEXT FOR READING

Thinking About the Big Ideas   Ask students what *seeds of conflict* means. Encourage them to draw on their own knowledge to demonstrate that conflicts have underlying causes that may date back many years. Read aloud the John Adams quote above, and ask students what Adams believed was the underlying cause of the American Revolution. *(a radical change in the hearts and minds of the people)*

Drawing Inferences from Pictures   Invite students to preview the pictures in Chapters 1-6. Ask what they can infer about the kinds of people who played important roles in American history during this period. *(British officials and soldiers, Native Americans, and colonial leaders as well as everyday citizens)*

SETTING A CONTEXT IN SPACE AND TIME

Using Maps   On the world map in the Atlas, have students locate England, France, and North America. Then have students switch to a map of North America and indicate the geographic area covered by Part 1. Ask students to identify modern place names in this area. *(Canadian provinces, eastern U.S. states, major landforms)* If any students have visited these areas, encourage them to tell of their experiences: the cities, the landscape, the variety of people, and so on. Ask students to retell important things they have learned up to this point about the history of these areas. List their responses on the board.

Understanding Chronology Have students turn to the Chronology of Events on page 202 and identify the events of 1735-1763. What major conflict affected North America? *(British versus French for control of North America)* Who won this conflict? What events support this answer? *(England; British victories)* Turn attention to the events after 1763. What new conflict is arising because the British defeated the French? *(between the British and their American colonies)*

NOTE TO THE TEACHER

When you see the instruction "Read...," you can interpret it in any way that fits the lesson you are creating for your students. For example, you may read aloud to the class or to small groups, you may have volunteers read aloud, or you may have the class read silently.

READING NONFICTION

Analyzing Rhetorical Devices

Andrew Hamilton was a master of persuasion. Have students list on the board "loaded words" (words with positive or negative connotations that create strong emotions) from his speeches that would have special influence on the jury. (*free men, oppose arbitrary power, truth, blessings of liberty, cause of liberty*) Have students evaluate the effect of using such words.

GEOGRAPHY CONNECTIONS

On the world map in the Atlas, have students locate Germany. Then have them trace the route that the boat bearing Zenger and his family might have taken to America in 1710. Remind students that overcrowded, creaky sailing ships were then the only means of making such a trip and that the trip could take many weeks. Ask students how such a journey at age 13 might have influenced Zenger. (*It must have steeled him against hardship and taught him to be patient.*)

MORE ABOUT...

Zenger's Trial

Zenger did not testify at his trial. Obviously, this did not hurt his defense, as the jury took only 10 minutes to reach their resounding verdict of "not guilty."

NOTE FROM THE AUTHOR

I try to give my readers facts and ideas and let them argue about them. And after they get into the material, they seem to do just that. The most passionate discussions we have are often about politics. Well, history is just the politics of the past.

1 Class Period   Homework: Student Study Guide p. 11

Chapter Summary

The trial of Peter Zenger galvanized the colonists and laid the foundation for two fundamental principles of liberty in America: freedom of the press and trial by jury.

Key Vocabulary

apprentice	disbarred	arbitrary
libel	indentured servant	

1. CONNECT

Peter Zenger's trial, though it occurred nearly 300 years ago, is closely connected to the most important rights we enjoy today—freedom of speech, freedom of the press, and trial by jury. Ask students how their lives would be different if they did not have these rights. Help students recognize that Zenger's trial was the first American step on the road to securing these rights for all people.

2. UNDERSTAND

1. Read about Peter Zenger's apprenticeship on pages 13-14. Discuss: What experiences from Zenger's youth might have prepared him to become a serious workingman and eventually an American hero? (*Possible responses: his family's desire for freedom and opportunity; the loss of his father and his need to take on responsibility early; his seriousness in learning a trade*)

2. Read the rest of the chapter. Discuss: What were the important issues in the Zenger trial? (*the press's right to criticize government; government's power over the press; the role of a jury in a trial*)

3. CHECK UNDERSTANDING

Writing   Ask students to write a paragraph contrasting the government's argument against Zenger and Hamilton's defense of Zenger.

Thinking About the Chapter (Making Comparisons)   Call on volunteers to compare and contrast the relationship of the American press and the government in modern times with the relationship in Zenger's time. (*Today, the press may freely question and criticize government, and it is expected to do so; in Zenger's time, government could arrest members of the press for such criticism. Today, some media sources support the government and others do not, just as in Zenger's time.*)

JENKINS' EAR

PAGES 17-20

1 Class Period   **Homework: Student Study Guide p. 12**

Chapter Summary

When the Spaniards cut off Jenkins' ear, war was the result. The issue was not Jenkins' ear, but control of North America.

Key Vocabulary

people's war

1. CONNECT

The War of Jenkins' Ear was part of the competition among England, France, and Spain for control of North America. Call on students to use prior knowledge to locate on a wall map of North America where each of these nations exercised primary control. Call on volunteers to use current events to demonstrate that humans still have wars over territory (for example, in the Middle East, the Balkans, and Africa).

2. UNDERSTAND

1. Read pages 17 and 19 up to "The war was pretty much of a draw." Discuss: What was the immediate cause of the War of Jenkins' Ear? Was it a just cause or just a pretext? (*The punishment of a smuggler was just a pretext that England used to try to gain territory from Spain.*)
2. Read the rest of the chapter. Discuss: Why do you think being called "Americans" by the English soldiers marked a turning point for the colonists? (*The use of "Americans" marked a recognition that the colonists were a separate people from the English, that they had their own identity.*)

3. CHECK UNDERSTANDING

Writing   Ask students to write a short defense of one of these points of view—either "The War of Jenkins' Ear should have been fought" or "the War of Jenkins' Ear should not have been fought."

Thinking About the Chapter (Making Predictions)   Encourage the class to make predictions about what might lie ahead for England and their American colonists in relation to Spain and France. (*Students should recognize that more fighting lies ahead; for example, they know that Florida is now part of the United States, so it must have been won away from Spain.*)

READING NONFICTION

Drawing Conclusions

Have students read page 18 to understand the clash between the colonies of Georgia and Florida. Discuss why the two were "natural enemies." Encourage them to draw conclusions about why border wars are so common.

LINKING DISCIPLINES

Geography/Science

The text reports that yellow fever was a more potent killer than bullets in the War of Jenkins' Ear. Have volunteers research yellow fever, its causes and effects, and how it is linked to subtropical and tropical climates like that of Florida.

GEOGRAPHY CONNECTIONS

Have students use the top half of the reproducible blank US political comparison map to sketch and label English, Spanish, and French control of North America at the time of the War of Jenkins' Ear. Use maps on page 37 and in the Atlas to help draw and label boundaries. Have students keep this map in their history journals. They will complete it with the Part 6 Linking Geography and Politics activity.

GEOGRAPHY CONNECTIONS

The starting point for General Braddock's march was Fort Cumberland (now Cumberland, Maryland) just east of the Appalachian Mountains. Have students use a topographic map of the United States or the physical map at the back of the textbook to trace a possible route west through Virginia (now West Virginia) and into western Pennsylvania, and to determine why it took so long. (*The army had to cross heavily forested mountains.*)

MEETING INDIVIDUAL NEEDS

Visual learners might benefit by listening to the text description of Braddock's battle and picturing scenes from it in their minds. They might then draw their scenes and assemble them into a class book called *An Illustrated History of Braddock's Defeat.*

GEOGRAPHY CONNECTIONS

Colonial Era Map Activity

Have students begin the Colonial Era Map described on TG page 24. Have them locate and mark:

Ohio River	
Fort Cumberland	39°37'N 78°45'W
Fort Duquesne	40°26'N 80°01'W

1 Class Period   Homework: Student Study Guide p. 13

Chapter Summary

The French and Indian War determined the future of the continent. It also taught colonial leaders, such as George Washington, valuable lessons that would later help them shake off British rule.

Key Vocabulary

frontier   surveyor   musket

1. CONNECT

Have students recall which European countries were growing stronger in this period, and which were growing weaker. Then have them indicate on a wall map of North America or the map from the Chapter 2 Geography Connections activity the territory that Spain, England, and France claimed. Discuss why conflict between England and France would be more decisive for control of the continent than conflict between England and Spain.

2. UNDERSTAND

1. Read pages 21-23. Discuss: What caused conflict between the English and the French? (*Possible responses: claims to same land, religious and national differences, control of fur trade*) If you were a Native American, would you have fought for either side? Why or why not? (*Students should recognize the Native Americans' dilemma as they were losing their ancestral lands.*)
2. Read the rest of the chapter. Discuss: What effects do you suppose George Washington's first encounters with the French might have had on him? Why? (*Possible responses: He must have realized he had a great deal to learn about warfare; he saw that the European style of fighting was not effective in America.*)

3. CHECK UNDERSTANDING

Writing   Ask students to write a diary entry that Daniel Boone might have written after Braddock's defeat.

Thinking About the Chapter (Contrasting)   Have students complete a two-column chart contrasting the English/American forces with the French/Indian forces in clothing, use of environment, tactics, and results.

1 Class Period   **Homework: Student Study Guide p. 14**

Chapter Summary
An amazing English/Mohawk American named Warraghiyagey (William Johnson) helped turn the course of the French and Indian War in favor of the British. Contact with the Iroquois League also fueled visions of union in the minds of colonists such as Ben Franklin.

Key Vocabulary
feudal lord   sachem   baronet

1. CONNECT

Write the chapter title on the chalkboard. Elicit students' thinking about what kinds of contributions remarkable figures can make to society. Ask: What qualities do you think make someone "remarkable"? What American figures—historical or present—would you identify as remarkable? Why?

2. UNDERSTAND

1. Read to the end of the first paragraph on page 28. Discuss: Do you think the Mohawk name *Warraghiyagey* fit William Johnson? Why? *(The name means "he who does much." It fits Johnson because he did many things for many people, both Native American and European. Students should include some of his achievements.)*
2. Read the rest of the chapter. Discuss: How did Warraghiyagey change the course of the French and Indian War? *(He convinced the Iroquois to fight on the side of the British, which helped to bring on a French defeat.)*

3. CHECK UNDERSTANDING

Writing   Ask students to write a short biographical sketch of William Johnson.

Thinking About the Chapter (Evaluating)   Encourage students to identify and evaluate the importance of the Iroquois League. On the chalkboard, write *Iroquois* and *In union there is strength*. Have students discuss how the Iroquois Confederacy exemplifies this saying and why the Confederacy appealed to colonists like Ben Franklin.

HISTORY ARCHIVES
A History of US Sourcebook
#9, From Benjamin Franklin, *Poor Richard's Almanack* (1733)

MEETING INDIVIDUAL NEEDS
Students interested in Native American history might research the formation of the Iroquois League. Ask them to investigate the fascinating mystic Deganawidah, whose proselytizing helped bring the League into being. Encourage students to present the story to the class.

MORE ABOUT...
Albany Congress
The example of the Iroquois League had a profound effect on Ben Franklin and his hopes for colonial unity. The plan for uniting the colonies that he proposed at Albany came to be called the Albany Plan of Union. Historians generally mark it as one of the earliest seeds of the modern American governmental system.

ACTIVITIES/JOHNS HOPKINS TEAM LEARNING
See the Student Team Learning Activity on TG page 34.

MORE ABOUT...

The Plains of Abraham

The Heights of Abraham led to a flat area behind Quebec called the Plains of Abraham, where the Battle of Quebec was fought. These names sound as though they have Biblical origins. Actually, the area was named for Abraham Martin, a pioneer who had settled there. As the owner of this site, he grazed his sheep on it.

LINKING DISCIPLINES

History/Art

Turn to the painting *Death of General Wolfe* on page 32, and explain that it was completed in 1771, 12 years after the battle. The painter was Benjamin West, a renowned American artist, who was at the time of the battle only 19 years old and living in Philadelphia. Explain that the painting is in a long tradition of historical paintings that glorify events their artists never witnessed. Have students discuss how true-to-life they think this scene might be. Remind them that there were no photographers at the time.

GEOGRAPHY CONNECTIONS

Have students use the map and chart on page 33 to pose and answer questions about the geographic patterns shown. Using the chart and map together, students can pose and answer questions such as: Where were the early battles fought, to the north or to the south? What major rivers were involved in the conflict? Were more battles fought near English settlements or French settlements?

GEOGRAPHY CONNECTIONS

Colonial Era Map Activity

Have students continue the Colonial Era Map described on TG page 24. Have them locate and mark:

Quebec	46°48'N 71°23'W
Montreal	45°28'N 73°45'W

CHAPTER

5 PITT STEPS IN

PAGES 31–33

1 Class Period   Homework: Student Study Guide p. 15

Chapter Summary

With the help of the colonists and their Native American allies, the British won the French and Indian War. But another conflict soon arose over who should pay for the war.

Key Vocabulary

foreign secretary   diplomat

1. CONNECT

Have students list the advantages that the French and the English had in a war in North America. Ask them to draw a conclusion as to which colonial power would be more likely to win based on these advantages.

2. UNDERSTAND

1. Read the chapter. Discuss: What was General Amherst's view of the American colonists? (*Amherst had nothing but contempt for them, and felt they were inferior to English people.*)
2. Ask: How did the French and Indian War solve one conflict for the British while adding fuel to another? (*The British wrested control of eastern North America from the French, but having to pay the costs of war created problems between the English and the colonists.*)

3. CHECK UNDERSTANDING

Writing Ask students to write a news report about the Battle of Quebec, foreshadowing the end of the French and Indian War.

Thinking About the Chapter (Drawing Conclusions) Encourage students to study the map on page 33. Have them note that most of the battles were fought near rivers or lakes. Ask them to draw conclusions about the importance of water routes at that time from this information.

6 AU REVOIR (GOODBYE), FRANCE

PAGES 34-35

1 Class Period   **Homework: Student Study Guide p. 16**

Chapter Summary

The spoils of war went to Great Britain. For their support, the Iroquois got nothing. Worse yet, land-hungry colonists cast their eyes on Indian lands west of the Appalachians.

Key Vocabulary

mission   presidio

1. CONNECT

Read the chapter title to students, and make sure they all understand that *au revoir* is French for "goodbye." Students should recognize that this means not only that France lost her North American colonies, but also that her influence over the development of the future United States was virtually at an end.

2. UNDERSTAND

1. Read the chapter. Discuss: After 1763, which colonial powers were left in North America? *(England and Spain)*
2. Ask: How would you describe the situation of the Native Americans after the war ended? *(They no longer were needed as allies by the English. They lost their great trade partner in the French. Their lives were threatened by disease, and their lands continued to be taken away.)*

3. CHECK UNDERSTANDING

Writing   Ask students to write a paragraph explaining who they think were the big winners and the big losers of the French and Indian War.

Thinking About the Chapter (Categorizing)   Have students complete a two-column chart on the chalkboard contrasting Sir Jeffrey Amherst's attitudes toward Native Americans with those of Sir William Johnson. Students should include details supporting their ideas.

LINKING DISCIPLINES

History/Literature

Longfellow's poem "Evangeline" tells the story of the exile of the Acadians from Canada. Encourage a group of volunteers to prepare a presentation of it for the class. A narrator can research and set the historical stage for it, and the others can perform the dramatic reading.

GEOGRAPHY CONNECTIONS

To help students summarize the huge change in power that took place in 1763, have them complete Resource Page 1 (TG page 109). They may use a map of North America and their textbooks to complete the activities.

JOHNS HOPKINS TEAM LEARNING

INTERPRETING POLITICAL CARTOONS

1 CLASS PERIOD

FOCUS ACTIVITY

1. Bring in a variety of political cartoons clipped from newspapers or ask students to bring them in. Divide the class into teams, and distribute copies of the cartoons to the teams.

2. Working with their teammates, have students examine the political cartoons to discover and identify symbols that political cartoonists use and how they use them.

3. Teams should use **Roundtable** to brainstorm how symbols can convey a political cartoonist's opinion or idea in brief and graphic fashion.

STUDENT TEAM LEARNING ACTIVITY/IDENTIFYING SYMBOLS AND MEANING

1. After students have read Chapter 4, refer them to the "Join or Die" cartoon on the first page of the chapter. Let them know that this cartoon first appeared in *The Pennsylvania Gazette* on May 9, 1754 and that within a month, virtually every newspaper in the colonies had reprinted it. Post these questions about the cartoon on the board for teams to answer:

- *Who is the cartoonist?*
- *What have you learned that he wanted the colonies to do in 1754?*
- *What is the major symbol the cartoonist used?*
- *What did he do to it to create smaller symbols? What do they symbolize?*
- *How would you put in words the message of this cartoon?*
- *How effective do you think this cartoon is in making its point to people? Why?*

2. Circulate and Monitor As the teams work, visit with them to answer any questions and to keep them on track.

3. Use **Numbered Heads** to have the teams share their answers to the questions. Then encourage the class as a whole to discuss the cartoon's style and effectiveness. Help them to see how powerful simplicity can be in conveying an idea. To underscore the effectiveness of the cartoon in its time, let them know that it would be reprinted time and again in the two decades after its first appearance.

ASSESSMENT

SUMMARIZING PART 1

Part 1 Check-Up Use Check-Up 1 (TG page 102) to assess student learning in Part 1.

ALTERNATE ASSESSMENT
Ask students to write an essay answering one of the following questions, which link the big ideas across chapters:

1. Making Connections How did each of the following reflect changing attitudes in the colonies or Great Britain: the trial of Peter Zenger, use of the term *American*, the French and Indian War? *(Zenger trial: a willingness by colonists to defend their rights and challenge arbitrary power; differing concepts of libel emerged in the colonies. Use of* American: *rise of a national identity separate from England. French and Indian War: taught colonists lessons about war and British weaknesses; planted seeds of future conflicts over western settlement and repayment of war debts.)*

2. Making Connections Why did some Native Americans side with the French while others sided with the English during the French and Indian War? *(Students should recognize that while French use of the land was more in keeping with Native American use, and that therefore the French were a more natural ally, Champlain's earlier alliance with the Algonquins against the Iroquois turned the Iroquois against the French.)*

DEBATING THE ISSUES
Use the topics below to stimulate debate.

1. Resolved That Peter Zenger should be found guilty as charged. (Remind students that they must take either the British or the colonial point of view. Encourage them to find all the reasons and details they can to support their argument.)

2. Resolved That British colonists had a right to settle on land west of the Appalachians. (You may want to organize this debate as a panel discussion. Each panel member should represent one of the following points of view: English colonist, British official, Native American, Spanish colonist.)

MAKING ETHICAL JUDGMENTS
The following activities ask students to consider issues of ethics.

1. Have students reread the words of Andrew Hamilton on pages 15 and 16. Why do you think that Hamilton believed Zenger's case was so important? Do you believe that the right to "speak and write truths" is that important? (Students should consider what it is like to live in a society in which freedom of speech and of the press are denied and how those restrictions rob citizens of individual liberty and of the power to oppose the government.)
2. Benjamin Franklin and William Johnson held views about

USING THE RUBRICS
To assess these writing assignments, group projects, and activities, scoring rubrics have been provided at the back of this Teaching Guide. Be sure to explain the rubrics to your students.

Analyzing a Poem

Read aloud the following poem, written by Ben Franklin in 1763.

> *Know ye, bad neighbors, who aim to divide*
> *The sons from the mother, that she's still our*
>   *pride,*
> *And if you attack her, we're all on her side,*
> *Which nobody can deny, deny.*

Ask students what they can infer from the poem about what Franklin thinks about the ties between the colonists and England in 1763. *(They are still close.)* What hints does Part 1 give about conflict that might strain these ties? *(colonial interest in western lands; British belief that the colonists should help pay for the costs of empire)* Tell students that they will explore these and other conflicts in Part 2.

Native Americans that were different from many of their fellow colonists. Imagine that you are one of these men and explain why you believe as you do. What arguments would you raise against colonists who are prejudiced against Native Americans? (Students should recognize that these two men had the wisdom to understand and to value people and ways of life that were different from their own.)

PROJECTS AND ACTIVITIES

Writing News Stories Assign students to write news stories about the Zenger trial for a colonial newspaper such as the *Pennsylvania Gazette*. Encourage students to take a pen name to protect them from arrest by British authorities. The stories should answer as many of the reporter's questions as possible: *Who? What? When? Where? Why? How?*

Reenacting History Have the class divide into groups to design short skits reenacting the Zenger trial. Encourage students to include quotes from Chapter 1 in the dialogue. As each group presents its skit, have the rest of the class take notes on the main points presented by the actors. In a follow-up discussion, ask: What points did each skit emphasize? In what, if any, ways did the skits depart from history?

Designing Storyboards Have students design storyboards for the War of Jenkins' Ear. Each frame should show a major event leading up to the war and the war itself. Students should design their frames in miniature, and then make final copies for display on newsprint or poster board.

Analyzing a Quote Read aloud the following statement from a letter sent to Great Britain by an Oneida chief named Scarouady:

> *Those that come over the great seas…are unfit to fight in the woods. Let us go ourselves…to conquer the French.*

Ask: What information in Chapter 3 explains this request by a chief of the Iroquois League?

Using Historical Information Have students work in small groups to devise oral histories that an Iroquois grandparent might have told his or her grandchild about the feats of War-raghiyagey. Allow time for "grandparents" to share their oral histories with the class.

Drawing an Illustrated Historical Map Using an opaque projector, have students draw a large version of the map on page 33 on sheets of poster board or newsprint. Then assign groups of students to make spot illustrations for the map for each of the battles shown on the time line. Encourage them to use encyclopedias or books on the French and Indian War to research uniforms and geographic locations. Remind students that pictures in the text also serve as a source of information.

THE BIG IDEAS

In the closing months of the French and Indian War, an English clergyman named Andrew Burnaby toured the colonies. He formed a picture of 13 jealous, squabbling governments. In 1760, he wrote:

> Nothing can exceed the jealousy...which they possess in regard for each other....[W]ere they left to themselves, there would soon be a civil war from one end of the continent to the other....

Burnaby failed to see that common ideals and beliefs tied the colonies together or that these ideals would change bickering colonists into American patriots. Part 2 describes the spirit of independence that helped fuel conflict with the home country.

PART 2

BLAZING NEW TRAILS

INTRODUCING PART 2

SETTING GOALS

Introduce Part 2 by writing its title on the board—*Blazing New Trails*. Ask students to conjecture about what new trails the colonists will be blazing. Help them see that besides trails west, colonists will blaze new trails in their relations with Britain.

To set goals for Part 2, tell students that they will
- explain why the colonists moved toward independence.
- understand the character traits of an "American."
- recognize the effects that expanding colonial settlement was having on Native Americans.
- list "rights of Englishmen" the colonists would demand.

SETTING A CONTEXT FOR READING

Thinking About the Big Ideas   To get students thinking about the colonies becoming less dependent on England, ask them about changes they have experienced while growing up. Ask: How will you become more independent in the years ahead?

READING NONFICTION

Making Inferences   This Part discusses the "new American" that was developing in the English colonies. Have students create a two-column chart with the headings *Observation* and *Character Trait.* As they skim or read the chapters, have them jot down in the first column the various observations that are made about the American colonists. Then have them infer the national character trait that each observation illustrates.

SETTING A CONTEXT IN SPACE AND TIME

Using Maps   Refer the class to the map on page 37 to see how British territory in North America has grown. Invite them to speculate why this larger territory may be more difficult to govern.

Using Time Lines   Tell students that their time lines are going to become very crowded. They may want to choose a symbol such as a firecracker to indicate milestones on the road to independence.

The Great Awakening

Explain that some historians believe that the Great Awakening helped stoke the fires of independence. Ask students what connection they can see between a religious revolution and a political revolution. Help them to see that the Great Awakening taught colonists to question traditional authority and loyalties.

GEOGRAPHY CONNECTIONS

Refer the class to the map on page 37 and have them locate and identify the two major rivers of the western lands. (*the Ohio and the Mississippi*) Ask students why such waterways might be helpful to pioneers. (*transportation, rich farm land*) Also call their attention to the Appalachian Mountains. Have them explain why finding gaps in these mountains was so important. (*Otherwise, settlers would not be able to get their wagons through the mountains.*)

GEOGRAPHY CONNECTIONS

Colonial Era Map Activity

Have students continue the Colonial Era Map described on TG page 24. Have them locate and mark:

Mississippi River

Appalachian Mountains

Proclamation Line of 1763

CHAPTER **7** | STAYING IN CHARGE

PAGES 36-38

1 Class Period   Homework: Student Study Guide p. 17

Chapter Summary

Great Britain tried to control the westward movement of colonists with the Proclamation of 1763. But independent-minded pioneers like Daniel Boone had no intention of following orders from faraway England.

Key Vocabulary

Great Awakening   proclamation   speculator

1. CONNECT

Read the chapter title aloud. Encourage students to use what they have learned to say why Britain might find it increasingly difficult to stay in charge of the American colonists.

2. UNDERSTAND

1. Read pages 36-37. Discuss: What seeds of conflict would be found in the lands west of the Appalachians? (*conflict between would-be settlers and the British government, as well as between settlers and Native Americans who lived there*)
2. Read the rest of the chapter. Ask: Why did so many colonists want to move west of the Appalachians? (*Eastern lands were mostly taken; speculators wanted the land; people were hungry for land.*) What two routes did early pioneers take? Where did they settle? (*cross the mountains to Pittsburgh, and then take the Ohio River to the Ohio River Valley; Wilderness Road through the Cumberland Gap to Kentucky*)
3. The Daniel Boone quote on page 38 comes from *The Adventures of Daniel Boone*, published in London in 1792. Resource Page 2 (TG page 110) contains more material about Boone's adventures. Give students copies so they can discover why the wilderness had such a hold on Boone.

3. CHECK UNDERSTANDING

Writing   Write a paragraph explaining what the British would have to do to enforce the Proclamation of 1763.

Thinking About the Chapter (Speculating)   Have students use what they know about the American colonists and what they have learned in this chapter to list grievances the colonists will have against the British resulting from the Proclamation of 1763. (*Students should include grievances that would result from the British enforcing the proclamation, such as throwing settlers off the western lands; protecting the enemy—Native Americans; denying their right to seek land of their own, and so on.*)

8

WHAT IS AN AMERICAN?

PAGES 39–41

1 Class Period   **Homework: Student Study Guide p. 18**

Chapter Summary

Even before the Revolution, Hector St. John Crevecoeur sensed the creation of a new people called "Americans." Their society combined a unique blend of English liberty with a sense of freedom and opportunity spawned by a vast frontier.

Key Vocabulary

yeoman   farmers   posterity

1. CONNECT

Remind students that although the 13 colonies are called *English colonies,* not all people living there had English ancestry. Ask them to recall what other groups had come to these colonies. *(Dutch in New York and New Jersey, Germans and others in Pennsylvania, Africans in various colonies, and so on)* Discuss how living in proximity to people from different backgrounds might change each group, resulting in a new culture for all.

2. UNDERSTAND

1. Read the chapter. Discuss: How would you contrast what Europeans expected in life with what Americans expected? *(Possible contrasts: rule by aristocrats vs. individual liberty, limited possibility of land ownership vs. owning one's own farm)*

2. Have volunteers reread aloud how Crevecoeur answered the question "What is an American?" (page 40). Discuss: How is Crevecoeur's definition of an American a recipe for change? *(New circumstances are helping develop a new culture, with new ideas, and it will no longer fit itself to the expectations, laws, and governments of the past.)*

3. CHECK UNDERSTANDING

Writing   Ask students to write a one-paragraph summary in their own words of Crevecoeur's definition of an American.

Thinking About the Chapter (Confirming Predictions) Read Crevecoeur's prediction: *Here individuals of all nations are melted together into a new race of men, whose labors and posterity will one day cause great change in the world.* Encourage students to use what they know to evaluate the accuracy of Crevecoeur's prediction.

READING NONFICTION

Analyzing Text Features

Call students' attention to the way the text on page 40 is organized: the author introducing main points in regular text, followed by Crevecoeur's words from *Letters From an American Farmer* in italics. Have students point out sentences that begin with the author's words and end with Crevecoeur's words. Elicit from students possible reasons the author used this organization, and how effective they think it is. *(She is highlighting Crevecoeur's most important ideas, and then using his words to support the ideas.)*

LINKING DISCIPLINES

History/Science

Call students' attention to the American Pie feature on page 40. Ask: Why would colonists take such time and trouble to dry fruit? *(Students should realize that there was no refrigeration at the time. People had to find ways to preserve their harvests so they would have food year-round.)* Ask a team of volunteers to investigate the principles of food dehydration, including why it preserves food, and report their findings to the class.

HISTORY ARCHIVES

A History of US Sourcebook

1. #9, From Benjamin Franklin, *Poor Richard's Almanack* (1733)

2. #18, From J. Hector St. John de Crevecoeur, *"What Is an American?": Letters from an American Farmer,* Letter III (1782)

ACTIVITIES/JOHNS HOPKINS TEAM LEARNING

See the Student Team Learning Activity on TG page 42.

MEETING INDIVIDUAL NEEDS

To reinforce understanding of colonial class structure, visual learners might use the description on page 42 to create a diagram of the classes in descending order.

LINKING DISCIPLINES

History/Science

Eliza Lucas Pinckney experimented with silk production. Since then, many attempts have been made to establish silk production in the United States, with little success. Call on volunteers to investigate the requirements of silk production and why it has failed here. They can also investigate how the gypsy moth infestation is connected to attempts at silk production. Have researchers present their findings to the class.

ACTIVITIES/JOHNS HOPKINS TEAM LEARNING

See the Student Team Learning Activity on TG page 42.

CHAPTER 9 — A GIRL WHO ALWAYS DID HER BEST
PAGES 42–45

1 Class Period   Homework: Student Study Guide p. 19

Chapter Summary

Eliza Lucas showed how the colonial experience changed the world. In an era when women had few rights, Eliza carved out a role as a scientist and business manager.

Key Vocabulary

indigo   Founding Mother

1. CONNECT

Discuss why developing a wide range of skills was essential to colonists. *(Many had to grow their food, sew their clothing, build their houses, and so on.)* Encourage students to discuss the positive images of hard workers we have in our popular culture today to help them see that hard work has been a core American value since the beginning.

2. UNDERSTAND

1. Read pages 42-44 up to "In the meantime, her father...." Discuss: How many different skills did Eliza Lucas develop and how did they contribute to her independent spirit? *(As students name the great variety of skills, list them on the board. Students should make the connection between developing these skills and becoming an independent, self-confident person.)*
2. Read the rest of the chapter. Discuss: Would you say that Eliza Lucas Pinckney is a fitting symbol for the spirit that was propelling the colonies toward independence? Why? *(She is a good symbol, for she thought for herself, took care of herself, and felt her future was in her own hands.)*

3. CHECK UNDERSTANDING

Writing   Have students reread Scoured the Pewter on page 43. Ask them to write a similar "Day in the Life of Eliza Lucas Pinckney."

Thinking About the Chapter (Hypothesizing)   Encourage students to hypothesize about what position a woman like Pinckney might hold in the United States today, and explain their reasons.

1 Class Period   Homework: Student Study Guide p. 20

Chapter Summary

English settlers were no strangers to conflict in the name of liberty. The cornerstones of English government were forged out of conflicts between the English people and their rulers.

Key Vocabulary

Glorious Revolution   Magna Carta   writ
Bill of Rights   *habeas corpus*   constitution

1. CONNECT

Remind students of the Zenger trial they studied in Chapter 1. Ask them to review the rights it dealt with: free speech, free press, trial by jury. Elicit that, although modern Americans have these rights automatically, they had to be hard-won.

2. UNDERSTAND

1. Read about the Magna Carta and the rights of English citizens on pages 46-48. Discuss: Why did the English come to believe that they needed protection against their monarch? *(Their monarch had the power of life and death over them. King John, abused the power so terribly that the barons rose against him.)* What rights that we have now were first guaranteed by the Magna Carta? *(trial by jury, habeas corpus, no self-incrimination)* How did writing these down protect the people from evil government actions? *(It meant that the monarch—or the government—no longer had absolute power over the people.)*
2. Read the rest of the chapter. Ask: How did the Glorious Revolution change the balance of power between monarch and the people? *(It made the people, through their representatives in Parliament, more powerful than the monarch.)*

3. CHECK UNDERSTANDING

Writing   Ask students to write a paragraph in which they explain why a written constitution promotes individual liberty.

Thinking About the Chapter (Analyzing)   Encourage students to discuss why the Magna Carta was a milestone in the long march toward democracy. *(Students should see it as a landmark in curbing the power of governments over the people they govern.)*

HISTORY ARCHIVES

A History of US Sourcebook
#8, From *The English Bill of Rights* (1689)

READING NONFICTION

Analyzing Word Choice

Have partners find words the author uses to describe the Magna Carta and the Glorious Revolution. *(one of the world's greatest documents of freedom; an important right; something revolutionary; especially glorious)* They should then write a sentence telling the author's point of view about these milestones in democracy.

MORE ABOUT...

Runnymede

An acre of Runnymede belongs to the United States. It was given to this nation after the assassination of President John F. Kennedy in 1963. There, a memorial dedicated by Queen Elizabeth II in 1965 proclaims:

This acre of English ground was given to the United States of America by the people of Britain in memory of John F. Kennedy, President of the United States....

Two more memorials mark Runnymede. One is for the British Commonwealth World War II dead. The other is from the American Bar Association commemorating the site as a source of the British-American legal tradition.

JOHNS HOPKINS TEAM LEARNING

WHAT IS AN AMERICAN?

1 CLASS PERIOD

JOHNS HOPKINS
U N I V E R S I T Y

FOCUS ACTIVITY

1. Divide the class into teams of four students each. Working with their teammates, have students decide "What is an American?"

2. Have teams use **Roundtable** to brainstorm characteristics of an American.

STUDENT TEAM LEARNING ACTIVITY/LOCATING, RECORDING, AND SHARING INFORMATION

1. Have teams divide into two partnerships. Each partnership should choose or be assigned either Hector St. John Crevecoeur's observations in Chapter 8 or Eliza Lucas Pinckney's life in Chapter 9. First, discuss with the class what characteristics are: traits or behaviors that people show through their actions; for example, independence or dependence, ambition or laziness, or willingness to try new things or reliance on tradition. Call on students to locate and record evidence of American characteristics that either Crevecoeur describes or Pinckney displays in her life.

Each partnership should create a graphic organizer such as a web to record the characteristics they identify as being typically American from Chapter 8 or 9. They should then use this information to create a small poster titled *An American Is...*

2. Sharing Information   When students are finished, each partnership should share their posters with the rest of the team. Each team should discuss the findings and arrive at a combined set of characteristics that they agree are typically American.

3. Circulate and Monitor   Systematically visit each team as the partnerships share their information. If necessary, help students locate characteristics they might have missed and check that the ones they have are accurate.

4. Have students use **Numbered Heads** to share information and arrive at a class-wide answer to the question "What is an American?"

ASSESSMENT

Part 2 Check-Up   Use Check-Up 2 (TG page 103) to assess student learning in Part 2.

ALTERNATE ASSESSMENT
Ask students to write an essay answering one of the following questions, which link the big ideas across chapters:

1. Making Connections   What conditions combined to help create the independent spirit of Americans? *(Students should cite such conditions as distance from Britain, mixing of people to create a new culture, the frontier, and the belief in individual liberty.)*

2. Making Connections   In the 1760s, a "push-pull" relationship existed between the colonies and Britain. Certain forces pushed colonists away from the home country. Other forces pulled them to think of themselves as English citizens. What are some of these push-pull forces? *(Push forces might include the lure of western land, a developing independent spirit, and denial of the idea of social classes. Pull forces might include the political heritage that shaped colonists' ideas of liberty.)*

DEBATING THE ISSUES
Use the topic below to stimulate debate.

Resolved   That the British had the right to close the West to settlement without the consent of the colonists. (Some students should argue that this was an example of the British government trampling on the colonists' rights as English citizens. Other students should argue that Britain was acting to defend and protect its colonies—a major investment and responsibility.)

MAKING ETHICAL JUDGMENTS
The following activities ask students to consider issues of ethics.

1. Suppose you were one of the 14 Iroquois leaders who joined Sir William Johnson in 1768 to hammer out a treaty with English-speaking settlers. Would you agree to sign a treaty turning over land west of Albany? Why or why not? (To help students with this question, you might request volunteers to create a mock dialogue in which Johnson and the Iroquois discuss the merits and faults of the proposed treaty.)

2. Even though the Proclamation of 1763 forbade settlers from moving west of the Appalachians, many did so anyway. Do you think they were right in doing so? Why or why not?

PROJECTS AND ACTIVITIES
Writing Historical Fiction   Have students individually or in small groups write a fictional account of one family choosing to head west beyond the Appalachians in 1763. Stories should

USING THE RUBRICS

To assess these writing assignments, group projects, and activities, scoring rubrics have been provided at the back of this Teaching Guide. Be sure to explain the rubrics to your students.

include reasons for moving, opinions of the Proclamation of 1763, and the route followed. Allow time for students to read their stories aloud.

LOOKING AHEAD

Analyzing a Quote

Tell students that as King George III plotted ways to take firmer control of the colonies, a member of Parliament named Edmund Burke gave him the following advice:

> We cannot, I fear...persuade them that they are not sprung from a nation in whose veins the blood of freedom circulates....An Englishman is the unfittest person on earth to argue another Englishman into slavery.

Call on students to summarize Burke's advice in their own words. Ask whether they agree or disagree with Burke. Then tell students that in Part 3 they will learn what happened when the king chose to ignore Burke's advice.

HISTORY ARCHIVES

A History of US Sourcebook
#1, *Magna Carta* (1215)
#4, *The Mayflower Compact* (1620)
#8, *From The English Bill of Rights* (1689)

Drawing Political Cartoons Refer students to the cartoon on page 38 and note techniques used by the cartoonist to poke fun at Franklin. Have students design a cartoon which criticizes colonists for unfair dealings and broken treaties with Native Americans. You might also tell students that Franklin was a skilled cartoonist in his own right. Suggest that interested students research and report on some of Franklin's cartoons.

Writing Book Reviews Divide the class into small groups. Have half the groups imagine they are reporters for a major London newspaper. The other half should act as reporters for various colonial newspapers. Assign at least one group of students to represent a struggling African American press. Challenge students to write a book review of a new book entitled *Letters of an American Farmer* by Hector St. John Crevecoeur.

Using Historical Evidence Read aloud the following passage from a letter written by Eliza Lucas to her father: "Won't you laugh at me if I tell you I am so busy in providing for posterity [the future] that I hardly allow myself time to eat or sleep." With the class, list evidence from the text supporting Eliza's claim. As a follow-up, have students use this evidence to complete Eliza's letter.

Analyzing Primary Documents Organize the class into three groups. Each group should use library and Internet resources to find out more about the significance of one of these documents: the *Magna Carta, The Mayflower Compact,* and *The English Bill of Rights.* Excerpts can be found in *A History of US Sourcebook.* Each group must present their findings to the others, using convincing points, illustrations/posters and other visual aids, and following written and oral language conventions. These presentations can be followed by a "Grand Discussion," in which the the students can compare and contrast. Rubrics for evaluating this project can be found in the back of this guide.

THE BIG IDEAS

In 1767, General Thomas Gage, commander-in-chief of British troops in North America, fired off a letter to one of his friends in Parliament:

The Colonists are taking great strides towards Independency; it concerns Great Britain by a speedy and spirited Conduct to shew them that these provinces are British Colonies dependent on her, and that they are not independent states.

Efforts to force the colonists into submission sparked a series of conflicts that paved the way to Lexington and Concord. Part 3 traces the events that provoked revolution. Stiff-backed British policies brought changes in the thinking of even moderate colonial leaders such as Pennsylvania's John Dickinson. "Heaven itself hath made us free," thundered Dickinson in 1768. Part 3 traces the events that provoked one of the most radical forms of political conflict—revolution.

PART 3
THE SPARKS OF WAR

INTRODUCING PART 3

SETTING GOALS

Encourage students to discuss what can happen in life when conflicts between people grow greater and greater. *(Possible outcomes: rifts between people, fights, divorce, all-out war)* Which seems to be the most likely outcome of the British-American conflict? *(war)*

To set goals for Part 3, tell students that they will
• describe the causes underlying the American Revolution.
• identify and describe the roles of major Revolutionary figures.
• contrast the goals of the British and of the Americans.
• describe the opening salvos of the American Revolution.

SETTING A CONTEXT FOR READING
Thinking About the Big Ideas With the class, brainstorm a list of taxes Americans pay today *(income, social security, property, sales, gasoline, school)*. Help students understand that, although most Americans recognize that taxes are needed to pay for desired government services, they still don't like to pay taxes. Then have students imagine how they would feel if they were not represented in the body that wrote the tax laws. Elicit that they would probably think the taxes were unfair, and that if such a situation continued, would protest or even fight to change it.

Categorizing Information To create a political continuum, draw a horizontal line on the board. At the left, write *Radical;* in the middle, *Moderate;* at the right, *Conservative.* Have students brainstorm characteristics of each political philosophy, and have students copy them on their papers. As you review the Part, have students add to or change their lists, and write down which leaders mentioned in the text fit which description.

SETTING A CONTEXT IN SPACE AND TIME

Using Maps   On a large map of the 13 colonies, have students locate the major cities of colonial America—including Boston, New York, Philadelphia, Williamsburg, and Charleston—and the distances between them. Elicit evaluations of the difficulty of overland travel in colonial times. Ask: Why might someone from Virginia be more likely to have a close connection with England than with Massachusetts? *(Besides explaining that sea travel was easier than overland travel, students should recognize that the colonies probably had stronger trade and cultural ties with England than with each other.)*

Thinking About Chronology   Explain that in this Part students will read about many events that took place in just 10 years—1765-1775. Help them understand the importance of this decade for the United States.

11 A TAXING KING

PAGES 50-55

1 Class Period   Homework: Student Study Guide p. 21

Chapter Summary

The British tried to raise revenues by imposing taxes on tea, every kind of printed matter, and a variety of other goods. Instead of paying the taxes willingly, the colonists sent the British a message: "No taxation without representation."

Key Vocabulary

Stamp Act   repeal

1. CONNECT

Ask students to use their personal experience to discuss ways people react when something valuable is taken away from them, especially without their consent. This is what happened—on a much larger scale—when Britain tried to take money from the colonists in the form of taxes.

2. UNDERSTAND

1. Read pages 50-53. Discuss: What did Britain do that angered the colonists? *(Britain levied taxes, wouldn't listen to colonial complaints, and sent troops to the colonies.)* What was the colonists' major reason for not paying the taxes? *(They were not represented in Parliament.)* Why did King George feel the colonists should pay? *(The taxes were to pay for foreign wars, including the French and Indian War.)*

2. After students read the margin note on mercantilism on page 53, ask them to analyze the conflict between Britain's and the colonies' application of the theory of mercantilism. Students should see that it was impossible for both Britain and the colonies to export more than they imported.

3. Read the rest of the chapter. Discuss: How did the British government's actions against the American colonists backfire? *(These actions heightened American feeling against the British and united colonists in their opposition.)*

3. CHECK UNDERSTANDING

Writing   Ask students to write a persuasive letter that John Rutledge might have sent to a Virginia newspaper.

Thinking About the Chapter (Hypothesizing)   Encourage the class to create a What Might Have Been flowchart. The first box should say, *Parliament levies taxes on colonies.* Have students fill in subsequent boxes assuming that Parliament tried something different to win the Americans over to their way of thinking. Finally, have them assess whether conflict could have been avoided.

READING NONFICTION

Analyzing Point of View

Refer students to the No Right to Tax feature on page 50. Ask: What is Pitt's viewpoint on Parliament taxing the American colonists? (*It shouldn't be allowed.*) Does Pitt use emotional or intellectual language to make his point? Explain. (*Intellectual; he points out that Parliament has never done this before, and that the colonial legislatures have always taxed themselves.*)

GEOGRAPHY CONNECTIONS

Colonial Era Map Activity

Have students continue the Colonial Era Map described on TG page 24. Have them locate and mark (Note: on reproducible map for this activity, locations for these cities are marked by dots):

Boston	42°15'N	71°00'W
New York	40°42'N	74°00'W
Philadelphia	40°00'N	75°00'W
Williamsburg, VA	37°15'N	76°37'W
Charleston, SC	32°52'N	80°00'W

Colonial Era/ Revolutionary War Room Map Activity

Have students begin the Revolutionary War Room map described on page 30. Have them locate and mark:

    Lexington/Concord

    Paul Revere's ride

Note: Although they are the opening acts of the Revolutionary War, these events precede the signing of the Declaration of Independence, so you may choose to consider them part of the Colonial Era Map.

HISTORY ARCHIVES

A History of US Sourcebook

#10, *Resolutions of the Stamp Act Congress* (1765)

1. #11, From Patrick Henry, *"Give Me Liberty or Give Me Death!": Speech to the Virginia Convention* (1775)

2. #12, *Memorial of the Presbytery of Hanover* (1776)

3. #13, From Thomas Paine, *Common Sense* (1776)

GEOGRAPHY CONNECTIONS

Distribute copies of Resource Page 3 (TG page 111) to give students further information about the road system in the colonies.

READING NONFICTION

Analyzing Text Organization

Elicit from students how the chapter is organized: after the introduction, each firebrand is discussed separately. This allows the reader to compare and contrast each personality. Have partners create a compare-and-contrast chart for Adams, Paine, and Henry using the following categories: *Background, Character Traits, Beliefs, Achievements*. Then have the class analyze their most significant similarities and differences.

MEETING INDIVIDUAL NEEDS

Invite students with an interest in public speaking to imagine that they are colonial firebrands. Ask them to develop short, fiery speeches to persuade their listeners that they must free themselves from British rule. Have them deliver their speeches to the class in stirring fashion.

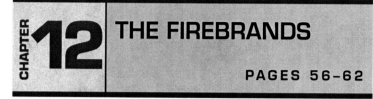

THE FIREBRANDS

CHAPTER 12

PAGES 56–62

1 Class Period   Homework: Student Study Guide p. 22

Chapter Summary

Three firebrands helped spark the American Revolution with their actions and words. From north to south, people soon knew the names Samuel Adams, Thomas Paine, and Patrick Henry.

Key Vocabulary

firebrand   committee of correspondence
deist

1. CONNECT

Get students thinking about the major causes of today—for example, saving the environment or ending tobacco use. What do people do to promote these causes? Help students recognize the strong need for persuasion, of using speaking, writing, or pictures to convince people to back each cause. This job faced colonists whose cause was revolution.

2. UNDERSTAND

1. Read the chapter. Discuss: What role did firebrands play in moving the American colonies to revolution? (*They were the persuaders, the ones who rallied other colonists to their cause.*) Why was this difficult to do? (*The colonists did not think of themselves as part of one country; poor transportation kept them separated; there was not much communication between colonies.*)

2. Ask: What were the special talents of Adams, Paine, and Henry? (*Adams: busybody, organizer, great thinker and writer; Paine: great writer; Henry: great speaker*) How was their message spread across the colonies? (*Adams started committees of correspondence; Paine published books; Henry spoke in the Virginia House of Burgesses.*)

3. CHECK UNDERSTANDING

Writing   Ask students to imagine that they are colonial firebrands. Have them write a broadside, or a one-sheet poster, calling for action against the British and why it should be taken.

Thinking About the Chapter (Hypothesizing)   Encourage students to tell which of the three firebrands—Adams, Paine, or Henry—would have been most persuasive to them had they been American colonists, and explain their reasons.

CHAPTER 13 — A MASSACRE IN BOSTON

PAGES 63-68

1 Class Period Homework: Student Study Guide p. 23

Chapter Summary
The Boston Massacre highlighted the rabble-rousing that fueled revolutionary sentiment. The conduct of John Adams in the trial that followed and the weighty questions considered by the Continental Congress showed the caliber of the colonial leaders.

Key Vocabulary
Quartering Act	redcoats	militia
deserters	Boston Massacre	Continental Congress

1. CONNECT

Discuss with students the nature of conflict and the way it can tend to build—from differing views to bad feelings to angry words and finally to violence. Encourage students to recall events in the conflict between British and Americans that match each of the first three steps.

2. UNDERSTAND

1. Read pages 63-66. Discuss: What happened as a result of the Quartering Act? (*In 1768, British fleet brought troops to Boston. Tensions rose between colonists and troops. In March 1770, these tensions flared into the Boston Massacre.*) Do you think the term *massacre* is accurate for what happened? (*Responses will vary.*)
2. Read the rest of the chapter. Discuss: What was the "big picture" that Adams saw? (*the chance to form a government based on fair-play and self-government*) Why was Adams's idea radical? (*Nowhere else did such a country exist.*) What were the important results of the First Continental Congress? (*resolutions concerning the rights of colonists; colonial leaders working together; petition sent to King George*)
3. Ask students how Congress's advice to stop buying British goods would conflict with Britain's mercantilism. Refer students to the margin note on page 53. (*By shifting the balance of colonial imports, the colonists would reduce Britain's financial gains.*)

3. CHECK UNDERSTANDING

Writing   Ask students to write a paragraph contrasting the characters of John Adams and his cousin Sam Adams.

Thinking About the Chapter (Analyzing)   Discuss what John Adams meant by, "The revolution was in the minds and hearts of the people." (*The people had to change their way of thinking before they moved toward freedom from Britain.*)

READING NONFICTION
Analyzing Primary Sources

Have students look at the illustrations on page 65. Ask them to analyze the propaganda value of these illustrations for the people of the time. (*They would make people angry at the British.*) Then have them use what the text says about the Boston Massacre to explain the care which we must use when working with primary sources.

MEETING INDIVIDUAL NEEDS

Visual learners might be encouraged to create their own illustrations of the Boston Massacre. They might aim either to produce a more realistic picture than Paul Revere's or one that tries to persuade viewers of just how evil the British are.

ACTIVITIES/JOHNS HOPKINS TEAM LEARNING

See the Student Team Learning Activity on TG page 52.

NOTE FROM THE AUTHOR

One teacher who piloted my books had her class turn the chapters into dramatic presentations. Groups of students were each given a different chapter. I happened by for a visit and saw some wonderfully free and imaginative presentations.

LINKING DISCIPLINES

History/Music

Help the class to work up a musical rendition of "Yankee Doodle" on page 74. If students do not know the melody, play a recording of it. Divide the class into groups and assign each group one of the choruses. Give them a little time to rehearse and then bring the class together to sing the song.

History/Literature

Using either a complete copy of Longfellow's "The Midnight Ride of Paul Revere" or the excerpts on pages 69, 73, and 75, help students work up a dramatic choral reading. Encourage them to stress the galloping rhythm of the poem.

GEOGRAPHY CONNECTIONS

Have small groups use the map on pages 70-71 to describe the routes followed by Revere, Dawes, and Prescott. You might suggest that students present their descriptions in the form of a dialogue in which the three riders tell each other about their journeys.

READING NONFICTION

Organizing and Interpreting Information from Reports
Have pairs of students research the Battle of Bunker Hill and report on the battle. One partner should report from the British point of view; the other from the American side. Stress the importance of students' organizing their information. They might make an outline with main ideas followed by details to support the ideas. Or they might create a chart of main ideas supported by details. When the reports are written, ask partners to exchange reports. Each partner should review and interpret the other's report. Suggest partners pose such questions as: What is the point of view? Is it supported by evidence? Has the reporter emphasized certain events and left out others? Has the reporter given a personal opinion rather than facts? Ask each pair to summarize its comments to present orally for class discussion.

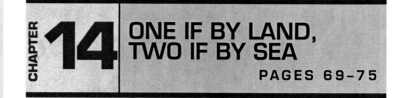

CHAPTER **14** ONE IF BY LAND, TWO IF BY SEA

PAGES 69-75

1 Class Period   Homework: Student Study Guide p. 24

Chapter Summary
Conflict turned into war when the minutemen and redcoats scuffled at Lexington and Concord. The march toward nationhood had begun.

Key Vocabulary
Patriot   Loyalist   minutemen

1. CONNECT

Remind students about the "people's wars" they read about in Chapter 2—how they were fought by popular leaders with the support of large numbers of people. Will the war they will read about in this chapter be such a war? Suggest that they read to find the answer.

2. UNDERSTAND

1. Read pages 69-73 up to "The American farmers were ready...." Discuss: Why was the work of Paul Revere and his colleagues so important to the infant revolution? *(They helped the underdog minutemen to fight successfully against a highly organized force of British professionals.)*
2. Read the rest of the chapter. Discuss: How do you think the battles at Lexington and Concord affected American colonists? *(Surely they must have heartened Patriots, to see that the British army was not invincible, and spurred them on. They must have disheartened the Loyalists, who saw the British bested and thus worried for their own safety.)*

3. CHECK UNDERSTANDING

Writing   Ask students to write a paragraph explaining whether they think the revolution will be a people's war.

Thinking About the Chapter (Evaluating)   Encourage the class to discuss Emerson's calling the first bullet fired at Lexington "the shot heard round the world." What did he mean? Do you think he was correct? Why or why not? Help the class to recognize that it was the opening salvo in a worldwide drive toward democracy that continues to this day.

CHAPTER 15 — AN AMERICAN ORIGINAL

PAGES 76-79

1 Class Period   Homework: Student Study Guide p. 25

Chapter Summary

The British possessed battle-tested generals. But the colonists boasted the raw courage of backwoods fighters such as Ethan Allen, who proved his daring with the capture of Fort Ticonderoga.

Key Vocabulary

Green Mountain Boys   Enlightenment

1. CONNECT

Refer the class to the chapter title. Encourage them to discuss what an *original* is, in terms of a human being. *(a singular human being, someone who is out of the ordinary)* Ask them what Americans, past or present, they might put in this category, and why.

2. UNDERSTAND

1. Read pages 76-78. Discuss: Why did the Patriots want to capture Fort Ticonderoga? *(to get its cannon for the American war effort)* Why do you think they chose Ethan Allen for the job? *(Students should describe his feistiness, daring, and courage, and his Green Mountain Boys.*
2. Read page 79. Discuss: Why do you think the Enlightenment was so important in making Americans seek self-government? *(It encouraged thinking for oneself rather than blindly following tradition; it stressed natural rights of people to govern themselves.)*

3. CHECK UNDERSTANDING

Writing   Ask students to write a one-paragraph biographical sketch of Ethan Allen.

Thinking About the Chapter (Synthesizing)   How was a drive for self-government both native to America and imported from Europe? *(Students should synthesize the Native Americans as self-governing tribes, the American colonists' independent spirit, and ideas from European thinkers.)*

MORE ABOUT...

Ethan Allen

Perhaps one reason Ethan Allen seemed always ready to pick up and join a fight was his first wife. She was noted in the community as being sour and bad-tempered. When she died, a man offered Allen help in transporting her coffin to the cemetery. He said to Allen, "There's not a man in town wouldn't be glad to help out." When Allen's own death seemed near, his doctor said to him, "General, I fear the angels are waiting for you." The crusty Allen replied, "Waiting, are they? Well—let 'em wait."

MEETING INDIVIDUAL NEEDS

You may wish to have some students research the life of Benedict Arnold, whose name is synonymous in American lore with the word *traitor*. Students with an interest in the personal side of history might like to investigate what propelled him to commit treason against the nation for which he had fought so well. Ask them to research Arnold and the reasons for his defection, and also what happened to him in the long run. Have these investigators present their findings to the class.

LINKING DISCIPLINES

History/Science

In their study of science, students have perhaps been introduced to scientific method—the steps scientists use in their research. This method grew out of the inquiring spirit of the Enlightenment. Run through the steps with the class: (1) recognizing a problem, (2) forming a hypothesis to explain it, (3) gathering data to test the hypothesis, (4) questioning the data and analyzing whether it proves or disproves the hypothesis, (5) drawing a conclusion. Encourage students to discuss why this is a sound method of investigation.

JOHNS HOPKINS TEAM LEARNING

THE BOSTON MASSACRE

1 CLASS PERIOD

FOCUS ACTIVITY

1. Ask students to recall TV news footage showing violence, mob action, or the taunting of police or military authority. Have them discuss the confusing nature of such incidents, and how difficult it is for even eyewitnesses to understand what is happening.

2. Students should consider how different eyewitnesses can relate conflicting accounts of what happened, depending on their vantage point and their opinion of the people involved. Have students make up examples of such conflicting accounts.

STUDENT TEAM LEARNING ACTIVITY/DIFFERENTIATING FACT AND OPINION; IDENTIFYING PROPAGANDA

1. Divide the class into teams of four students each. Working in partnerships, have the teams read the second and third paragraphs on page 65. As they note that the text says that the Paul Revere etching is "propaganda," explain the following points about propaganda.
• Propaganda is a technique of persuasion aimed at influencing individuals and groups.
• Propaganda is used to create a popular belief, true or not.
• Propaganda begins with a conclusion and then brings together any evidence that will support that conclusion and disregards information that will not.
• Propaganda must be simple, interesting, and credible to convince others.
Have the partnerships analyze Revere's etching, looking for means it uses to make one side look good and the other look bad, how it uses simplicity to make its point, and why it might be stirring to colonial people.

2. Circulate and Monitor Visit the teams and assist students in analyzing and discussing the etching and its propaganda techniques and value.

3. Have teams use **Numbered Heads** to report their findings to the class. Then encourage the class to discuss the etching as propaganda.

ASSESSMENT

Part 3 Check-Up   Use Check-Up 3 (TG page 104) to assess learning in Part 3.

ALTERNATE ASSESSMENT
Ask students to write an essay answering one of the following questions, which link the big ideas across chapters.

1. Making Connections   What three events do you think were most instrumental in pushing the American colonists toward war against the British? Explain why you chose each and how one might have been connected to another. *(Responses will vary, but students should give evidence of British absolutism and of the broad colonial desire to break away.)*

2. Making Connections   Of the figures you read about in this Part, choose one whose ideas reflected those of the Enlightenment and one whose ideas did not. Name each and explain why you chose that person. *(Responses will vary, but students should give evidence of one believing in the natural right to self-government and the other believing in the absolute power of a ruler over citizens.)*

DEBATING THE ISSUES
Use the topics below to stimulate debate.

1. Resolved   That Thomas Paine is right: "'tis time to part" from Great Britain. (To reflect a range of opinion, appoint some students to speak for the Loyalists. Others should speak for radical and moderate Patriots.)

2. Resolved   That the Patriots were justified in destroying tons of tea during the Boston Tea Party. (Appoint several students to speak for the East India Company. Mention that the right to private property was an important right protected by English law. Even some Patriots, including John Adams, questioned the tea's destruction.)

MAKING ETHICAL JUDGMENTS
The following activities ask students to consider issues of ethics.

1. John Adams infuriated his cousin Sam when John agreed to defend the redcoats involved in the Boston Massacre. Write a letter from John Adams to his wife Abigail in which he explains his reasons for representing the British soldiers. *(Letters should reflect Adams's Patriot sympathies but also his belief that self-government must rest on the rule of law rather than rule by mob.)*

2. How would you describe the ethical dilemma that faced the Americans and Native Americans in relation to each other? Where might you have stood in the matter? *(Encourage a freewheeling discussion that touches on such things as fairness, ideas*

USING THE RUBRICS

To assess these writing assignments, group projects, and activities, scoring rubrics have been provided at the back of this Teaching Guide. Be sure to explain the rubrics to your students.

about property rights, two groups desperately competing for the same thing, and two groups with different cultural values.)

PROJECTS AND ACTIVITIES

Writing Autobiographies   Assign students individually or in small groups to write a brief autobiographical statement for a figure they select from this Part. To get students started, write the following sentence frame on the chalkboard: *My name is _____, and I am important in history because _____.*

Making Decisions   With the class, brainstorm the various ways colonists could have protested the taxes enacted by Britain. Encourage students to go beyond the examples mentioned in the text. Have students work in teams to write short paragraphs in which they describe their method and give their reasons.

Writing Advertisements   Write the following incomplete advertisement on the chalkboard: *WANTED: Firebrand to work with Sam Adams and other Patriots in Boston. Candidate for the job must be _____.* Have students work in teams to complete the advertisement, focusing on the characteristics of firebrands mentioned in the text. Call on teams to read their ads aloud.

Planning a Trip   Have students pretend they are delegates headed to Philadelphia for the First Continental Congress. Have students refer to the feature on page 58 and write diary entries describing their method or route of travel.

Investigating Ideas   Divide the class into three groups. Assign each group one of the following headings: Enlightenment principles, English parliamentary traditions, Colonial (civic) republicanism. Have students brainstorm and research the headings to make a list of ideas and attitudes associated with each. Then have the groups present and compare their lists. After discovering similarities, have the groups make a large Venn diagram for the class bulletin board showing the overlap between the three ideas. As a class, discuss how these ideas set the stage for the first Continental Congress.

Identifying Points of View   Refer students to Who Started It? on page 70. Call on students to answer this question from the Patriot and British points of view. Then challenge students to draw sketches that the *Salem Gazette* and the *London Gazette* might have run to illustrate each account of the battles. You might post these sketches on the bulletin board.

LOOKING AHEAD

Stating the Problem

Read aloud the following selection from a letter written by John Adams to his wife Abigail. In it, Adams describes the task facing the Continental Congress.

> *When 50 or 60 men have a Constitution to form,...at the same time that they have a Country of fifteen hundred Miles extent to fortify, Millions to arm and train, a Naval Power to begin, an extensive Commerce [trade] to regulate,...a standing Army of Twenty seven Thousand Men to raise,...I really should pity 50 or 60 men.*

Based on this quotation, call on students to identify the problems facing the Patriots at the start of the American Revolution. Tell students that in Part 4 they will learn how the Patriots took steps to solve some of these overwhelming challenges.

THE BIG IDEAS

On June 7, 1776, Richard Henry Lee stood to address the Second Continental Congress. Although fighting raged in New England, the decision to declare independence still hung in the balance. Acting upon instructions from the Virginia assembly, Lee opened one of the great debates in our history. In ringing words, he declared:

> Resolved: that these United Colonies are, and of right ought to be, free and independent States, that they are absolved of all allegiance to the British Crown, and that all political connection between them and the States of Great Britain is, and ought to be, totally dissolved.

Seconded by John Adams, the resolution brought great changes. Delegates stopped talking about a struggle to win "the rights of Englishmen." Instead, they spoke of a revolution waged in defense of "natural rights." The job of defining these rights fell to Thomas Jefferson, author of the Declaration of Independence. Part 4 covers the chain of events that led Americans to adopt a new language of freedom.

INTRODUCING PART 4

SETTING GOALS

Write the Part title on the board, and beneath it draw a horizontal line representing a road. Ask volunteers to come to the board to enter important stops along the way that they have already investigated. *(Responses might include Proclamation of 1763, growing demand for rights of Englishmen, the various attempts to tax colonists, Boston Massacre, Boston Tea Party, Lexington and Concord, Ticonderoga.)* Help the class to see that conflict has grown upon conflict, and it will continue to do so.

To set goals for Part 4, tell students that they will
- identify the leaders of the Patriots.
- identify and describe the early battles of the American Revolution.
- explain the aims of the Declaration of Independence.
- explore the effects of the Declaration of Independence.

SETTING A CONTEXT FOR READING
Thinking About the Big Ideas   Challenge students to define the term *ideal*. *(a perfect model; a goal or principle)* Then request volunteers suggest some of the ideals associated with the United States. *(individual liberty, equality of opportunity, and so on)*

Next, read aloud the selection from the Declaration of Independence on page 99. Ask: What ideals are expressed in this passage? *(equality, liberty, possession of unalienable rights, government by consent of the governed)* Challenge students to summarize what ideal this document holds out for government, and why this was a radical change. *(one that protects the rights and liberties of its citizens; one that gets its power from the people; no government elsewhere in the world operated this way)*

Reading Primary Sources Many of the primary sources that Joy Hakim includes in this Part are composed in a very formal style that students rarely see in modern writing. Very often, sentences are much longer than they are today, with unusual punctuation and spelling, inversion, and archaic word meanings. You may wish to have small groups analyze particular pieces of writing to ensure their understanding of these timeless documents.

SETTING A CONTEXT IN SPACE AND TIME

Using Maps Have students locate Boston, Philadelphia, and Charleston on a classroom map. Discuss what a small area of the present United States the area they span represents, yet what an important role this area played in the nation's history.

Help students realize that although the focus of this Part is the 13 English colonies, the lives of Native Americans and Spaniards across the continent were also going on.

Understanding Chronology Ask students to turn to the list of events in 1775 on page 85. Discuss how a list like this helps readers understand the story of that time. Lead them in a discussion of how one event might affect a subsequent event; for instance, how the battles of Lexington and Concord in April would have affected the debates in the Second Continental Congress in May.

16 ON THE WAY TO THE SECOND CONTINENTAL CONGRESS   PAGES 80-84

1 Class Period   **Homework: Student Study Guide p. 26**

Chapter Summary
Few of the delegates who traveled to Philadelphia in 1775 wanted to rush headlong into revolution. However, with bullets flying in Boston, most wondered how long they could continue to call themselves English subjects.

Key Vocabulary
legislative authority   commonwealth

1. CONNECT

Point out that the founders of the American nation are admired as one of the finest collections of people ever assembled. They are revered for their intelligence, good sense, courage, and grasp of the "big picture." Invite students to name those they have already met and describe their achievements.

2. UNDERSTAND

1. Read the chapter. Discuss: On page 80, the author asks if we should make heroes of our politicians. How would you answer her questions? *(Use these questions to elicit a list of traits for the ideal politician. Use the list to "measure" the delegates.)*
2. Call on volunteers to name members of the Second Continental Congress, and list them on the board. Help students make generalizations about the type of people they were. *(In general, they were of European descent whose families had been in America for a long time. They were wealthy, well-educated and well-read, fine thinkers, and dedicated to the cause of independence.)* How would these characteristics tend to affect their work in the Congress? *(Responses will vary.)*
3. How many people did each delegate represent? Distribute copies of Resource Page 4 (TG page 112) and have them work with the figures given there.

3. CHECK UNDERSTANDING

Writing   Have students choose four figures from this chapter and write a descriptive sentence about each one.

Thinking About the Chapter (Synthesizing)   Have the class skim the chapter and pick out differences between the delegates. Ask: What effect do you think these differences might have had on their deliberations? *(The differences resulted in a number of perspectives in Congress, and strong debates over particular points.)*

MORE ABOUT...
The Virginia Lees
The Lee family of Virginia figures prominently in American history. Richard Lee settled in Virginia in about 1641, and soon became a wealthy planter and businessman. Two of his great-grandsons, Richard Henry Lee and Francis Light-foot Lee, served in the Continental Congress and signed the Declaration of Independence. Their cousin, Henry "Light Horse Harry" Lee, was a close friend of George Washington's and was a daring cavalry officer during the American Revolution. His son, Robert E. Lee, would become the most famous of all as the commander of the Confederate troops during the Civil War.

LINKING DISCIPLINES
Geography/Math
Divide the class into small groups, and assign each group one of the delegates. Have them identify his colony and find it on a map, and then use the map scale to estimate the distance he had to travel to Philadelphia. Students might also use the figures for stagecoach travel given on pages 57 and 59 (eight miles an hour, at best; eighteen hours a day) to estimate how long the trip would take.

MEETING INDIVIDUAL NEEDS
English language learners may have difficulty pronouncing the proper names in this chapter. Have students add brief entries and pronunciations to the class biographical dictionary.

GEOGRAPHY CONNECTIONS
As students work with Resource Page 4 (TG page 112), ask them to discuss the distribution of population among the colonies. Using the chart, have students work in pairs to pose and answer questions about distribution of population in the colonies. Students could ask, for example, whether all of the New England colonies had large populations (*no*), which colony had the largest population (*Massachusetts*), and so on.

 NAMING A GENERAL

PAGES 85-88

READING NONFICTION
Analyzing Rhetorical Devices

Have students reread the sidebar on page 88, and identify the play on words the author uses. (*body: meaning anybody and legislative body*) Remind students that the author uses humor often in the book, and one of the devices she uses is words with multiple meanings. Have students find other words in the text that have more than one meaning, and write sentences about the subject that contain plays on those words.

GEOGRAPHY CONNECTIONS

It was not only Washington's background and character that caused delegates to give him command of the Continental army. He also was from Virginia, the colony with the largest population. Ask students why this might have been a factor in his selection. (*The colony with the largest population was capable of providing the largest number of soldiers, and the army needed all the soldiers it could get.*)

MORE ABOUT...
Olive Branches

The olive branch has been a symbol of peace dating back to ancient times. According to Greek mythology, the goddess Athena gave the olive as a great gift to humankind. According to the Bible, an olive branch was the first vegetation Noah saw from the Ark, signaling the end of the flood. (The connection to peace was that olive oil could cure human ills and calm troubled waters.)

ACTIVITIES/JOHNS HOPKINS TEAM LEARNING

See the Student Team Learning Activity on TG page 63. Students should complete the activity before reading Chapters 18 and 19.

1 Class Period   **Homework: Student Study Guide p. 27**

Chapter Summary
The task of shaping raggedy militia into a Continental army fell to George Washington. Rejection of the Olive Branch Petition by King George III helped ensure that Washington would remain on the battlefield for nearly six years.

Key Vocabulary
Olive Branch Petition

1. CONNECT

Remind students that the Massachusetts militia had fought the battles of Lexington and Concord several weeks before the Second Continental Congress met. Elicit that these were local troops protecting their own land. What would Congress have to do militarily to win the War of Independence? (*create a national army; appoint a leader of all the troops*)

2. UNDERSTAND

1. Read pages 85-86. Discuss: How would the qualities Adams saw in Washington be useful for the leader of a Continental army? (*Students should recognize that having a military background as well as a character respected in all the colonies was crucial to success.*)

2. Read the rest of the chapter. Discuss: Why did Washington say that his appointment to command the American army would be the "ruin of my reputation"? (*This was an almost impossible task of leading the American army, with few guns, no cannons, and little training, against the imposing British army and navy.*) What does the fate of the Olive Branch Petition tell you about what is in store for the colonists? (*King George refused to read it, showing his unwillingness to compromise. Since the colonists were not backing down either, war was inevitable.*)

3. CHECK UNDERSTANDING

Writing   Ask students to imagine they are delegates to the Congress. Have them write a letter home describing Washington's selection and their hopes for the Continental army.

Thinking About the Chapter (Evaluating)   Call on the class to contrast Washington's leadership qualities with those of King George III. Which do they think had the greater chance of success in reaching his goals?

18 THE WAR OF THE HILLS

PAGES 89-93

1 Class Period   Homework: Student Study Guide p. 28

Chapter Summary

Battles at Breed's Hill and Bunker Hill introduced the redcoats to Patriot sharpshooters. The British pushed the Patriots off the hills, but only at a terrible cost of life.

Key Vocabulary

fortifications   barracks
earthworks   bayonet

1. CONNECT

Encourage students to review the battles of Lexington and Concord. Help them to see that this encounter was a "frontier" battle, with Patriots shooting from behind walls and trees and no set battle lines. Let the class know that they will now read about the first formal, pitched battle of the Revolution.

2. UNDERSTAND

1. Read pages 89-90 up to "If they had thought a minute…." Discuss: Reread the Pitcairn quote on page 89. Why do you think the British thought ending the Revolution would be easy? *(They assumed the Americans were lazy cowards, and that one good beating at the hands of the superior British army would make them give up.)* Why do you suppose the Patriots were able to fortify Breed's and Bunker hills so quickly? *(They had many people working together to fight for their freedom.)*
2. Read the rest of the chapter. Discuss: Who would you say won the battle of Breed's and Bunker Hills? *(The British captured the hills and chased the Patriots away, but it cost them many more men than the Patriots lost. The Patriots proved they could stand their ground against the British army.)*

3. CHECK UNDERSTANDING

Writing   Ask students to imagine that they had been a Patriot drummer boy on Breed's Hill. Invite them to write a paragraph-long diary entry describing their experience.

Thinking About the Chapter (Evaluating)   Ask students to describe American and British strategies in the battle: What was the goal of each side? How were they used to fighting? How successful were they? Ask students whether they agree with the quote on page 93 describing Bunker Hill as "a battle that should never have been fought on a hill that never should have been defended."

READING NONFICTION

Analyzing Point of View
Read aloud the sentence on page 93, "But what a price for two unimportant hills!" Ask students to interpret the author's point of view about the battle. *(She feels that the objective—taking two meaningless hills—was not worth the cost—more than 1,000 killed and wounded.)*

LINKING DISCIPLINES

History/Music
Refer the class to The Little Drummer Boy feature on page 92. Ask volunteers to research why armies of that time included drummer boys. *(Because of the noise of battle, voice commands often could not be heard, and so drums as well as fifes were used to issue orders such as Charge or Retreat. The instruments also helped the soldiers keep in step when they were marching in formation.)*

GEOGRAPHY CONNECTIONS

Resource Page 5 (TG page 113), The Battle of Bunker Hill, provides a graphic of the area involved in that conflict and asks students to use it and a text illustration to increase their understanding of that battle's logistics.

GEOGRAPHY CONNECTIONS

Colonial Era/ Revolutionary War Room Map Activity
Have students continue the Revolutionary War Room map described on TG page 24. Have them locate and mark:

    Breed's and Bunker Hills

Note: Although they are the opening battles of the Revolutionary War, these events precede the signing of the Declaration of Independence, so you may choose to consider them part of the Colonial Era Map.

MORE ABOUT...

Fort Moultrie

The fort on Sullivan's Island was originally called, not surprisingly, Fort Sullivan, but it was later renamed Fort Moultrie to honor Colonel William Moultrie. In the early 1800s, a new fort was built on the site by the U.S. government. In December 1860, the new Fort Moultrie was taken over by Confederate forces, and it was the headquarters for the Confederate bombardment of Fort Sumter, the military action that began the Civil War.

LINKING DISCIPLINES

History/Literature

Encourage students to perform a choral reading of the poem on pages 96-97, breaking it up into parts for different groups to read. Then invite the groups to write their own brief poems describing the battle, this time from the American perspective.

GEOGRAPHY CONNECTIONS

Colonial Era/ Revolutionary War Room Map Activity

Have students continue the Revolutionary War Room map described on TG page 24. Have them locate and mark:

Ft. Sullivan (Charleston, SC) 32°52'N 80°00'W

Note: Although a battle of the Revolutionary War, this precedes the signing of the Declaration of Independence, so you may choose to consider it part of the Colonial Era Map.

FIGHTING PALM TREES

PAGES 94-97

1 Class Period   Homework: Student Study Guide p. 29

Chapter Summary

When British ships attacked Fort Sullivan in Charleston Harbor in South Carolina, it seemed that even the trees fought back. Cannonballs stuck in the fort's soft palmetto wood, while Patriot cannons blasted the British ships.

Key Vocabulary

run aground   shoals

1. CONNECT

Ask the class to review how geography worked for the Patriots and against the British at Breed's and Bunker hills. (*The British had to march up the hills in the face of American fire raining down on them.*) Refer the class to the title of this chapter and invite them to speculate about how natural features might affect the battle they will read about here.

2. UNDERSTAND

1. Read pages 94-95. Discuss: In the battle of Charleston Harbor, how did geography work for the Americans and against the British? (*Native vegetation, in the form of palmetto logs, protected the American fort, and sandbars grounded British ships, making them easy targets.*)
2. Read the rest of the chapter. Discuss: How would you describe the feeling the British must have had as they left Charleston Harbor after the battle? (*Utter frustration and great anger, a blow to British pride and sense of invincibility. One British general called it "unspeakable mortification."*)

3. CHECK UNDERSTANDING

Writing Ask students to write a paragraph describing the Charleston battle from either the American or British point of view. Call on volunteers to read their paragraphs aloud to contrast the points of view.

Thinking About the Chapter (Hypothesizing) Ask students to imagine that they are the commander of the British fleet assigned to attack Charleston Harbor. What would they have done differently? (*Students should note the need to learn more about the harbor before sailing blindly into it, or to test the fort before mounting a frontal assault.*)

1 Class Period   **Homework: Student Study Guide p. 30**

Chapter Summary
The Declaration of Independence introduced the world to the American idea of democracy. Its lofty principles of equality and liberty have guided generations of Americans.

Key Vocabulary
declaration   consent of the governed

1. CONNECT

Call on students to recap what they have already learned about the independent spirit that the American colonists developed: their desire for personal freedom, their distaste for classes, their willingness to strike out on their own. What might be the next step for the colonies in their relations with Great Britain?

2. UNDERSTAND

1. Read pages 98-100. Discuss: Why do you suppose that the delegates wanted a declaration that was masterfully written? *(It not only had to make clear to the British what the Americans were doing, but it also had to make the case for independence and self-government in ringing tones to rally Americans to the Patriot cause.)*
2. Read the rest of the chapter. Discuss: How were some of the high ideals of the Declaration of Independence—such as "all men are created equal"—contradicted by society in America at the time? *(Slavery contradicted the Declaration's ideals, and many of the people who signed the Declaration were slave owners. Women were not allowed equal rights with men.)* Why didn't the Declaration mention slavery? *(Delegates from Georgia and South Carolina opposed Jefferson's words against slavery, so they were taken out in the name of unity.)*

3. CHECK UNDERSTANDING

Writing   Ask students to rewrite the excerpt from the Declaration on page 99 in their own words, reflecting what the word *men* should really refer to.

Thinking About the Chapter (Comparing and Contrasting)
Encourage students to contrast the status of women in the 1770s with their status today. Have them use the quotation from Jefferson on page 101 to investigate what even intelligent men thought of women then.

HISTORY ARCHIVES
A History of Us Sourcebook
#14, Thomas Jefferson, *The Declaration of Independence* (1776)

READING NONFICTION
Analyzing Rhetorical Devices
Refer the class to the All Men Are Created Equal feature on page 102. Invite them to write a paragraph in which they identify the bias that Benjamin Banneker is describing in his letter to Thomas Jefferson—who holds it and why it is unfair.

LINKING DISCIPLINES
History/Art
Refer the class to the political cartoon on page 100. Encourage them to brainstorm ideas for other actions that might symbolize a break—for example, running away from home, getting a divorce. Invite students to choose one of these symbolic actions and draw a political cartoon illustrating it. Advise them that they should make clear who is who and what action is taking place.

MORE ABOUT...
The Effects of the Declaration of Independence
When, in 1989, Chinese students poured into Tiananmen Square in China's capital of Beijing to demand political reform, they rallied support by reading aloud from the Declaration of Independence. They also carried signs bearing American slogans like *Give me liberty or give me death* and *Government of the people, by the people, and for the people.* Their final invocation of American ideals was their construction of a giant "Goddess of Democracy" statue in the square.

NOTE FROM THE AUTHOR

Is anyone in your class a stamp collector? Who are some of the people on U.S. commemorative stamps? Assign a stamp to each student and have them write a paragraph or page or essay about the stamp that can be read aloud to the rest of the class.

READING NONFICTION

Analyzing Word Choice

Ask students to find words and phrases that describe the consequences of signing the Declaration. ("vote away the blood and happiness of my countrymen," "pay with their lives," "fears and sorrows and sleepless nights") Ask students to discuss how these words strengthen the author's proposition that it took courage to sign the Declaration.

LINKING DISCIPLINES

History/Literature

Refer the class to An Awful Silence on page 105. Ask them to retell the joke that Colonel Benjamin Harrison made about his and Elbridge Gerry's fate. Explain that the literary term for this kind of joke is *gallows humor*. Help them understand that *gallows* refers to the frame used to hang people until they are dead, and then ask students why Harrison's joke is an example of gallows humor. (*It makes fun of a disastrous or life-threatening situation.*)

21 SIGNING UP

PAGES 103-105

1 Class Period   Homework: Student Study Guide p. 30

Chapter Summary

Today we call the delegates who signed the Declaration of Independence heroes. But King George III had another name for them—traitors.

1. CONNECT

On the chalkboard, write DECLARATION = DANGER. Ask students why this might be so. Danger to whom? Why? Encourage the class to speculate and then read the chapter to confirm or modify their speculations.

2. UNDERSTAND

1. Read pages 103-104. Discuss: Why did it take courage to sign the Declaration of Independence? (*Signatures branded the members of Congress traitors in the minds of the British. Such treason, if the Americans lost the war, would be punishable by death.*)
2. Read the rest of the chapter. Discuss: When King George heard about the Declaration of Independence, he remarked gloomily, "If it succeeds, none need call it treason." What do you think he meant? (*The label of traitor would stick only if the Patriots lost.*)

3. CHECK UNDERSTANDING

Writing   Ask students to imagine themselves delegates to the Congress. Have them write two lists—one of reasons they would want to sign the Declaration and one of reasons they would not want to sign it.

Thinking About the Chapter (Hypothesizing)   Point out that this chapter presents the Patriot point of view on the Declaration. Encourage students to hypothesize about the Loyalist point of view. (*To Loyalists, the Declaration must have seemed treasonous and highly threatening to them, their property, standing, and future.*)

JOHNS HOPKINS TEAM LEARNING

BATTLING FOR FREEDOM

1 CLASS PERIOD

FOCUS ACTIVITY

1. Have students **Brainstorm** ideas about what it must have been like to fight in the Revolutionary War, using illustrations in Chapters 18-19 for ideas. What weapons did the sides use against each other? How dangerous was fighting in lines, one side facing the other? What protections and advantages did fighting from forts offer?

2. In class discussion, have students **Speculate** about how they might want to fight if they were Revolutionary soldiers—in lines marching toward the enemy or from behind fortifications. Why? *(Fortifications offered something to hide behind and made it more possible to face a larger attacking force successfully.)*

STUDENT TEAM LEARNING ACTIVITY/LOCATING, RECORDING, AND SHARING INFORMATION

1. Divide the class into teams of four. In each team, one partnership reads Chapter 18 and the other reads Chapter 19. Ask the partnerships to write the following questions on a sheet of paper, with space below each, to create a reading guide. Instruct them to write answers for these questions as they read.
- Who was fighting whom?
- What was each side trying to accomplish?
- Where did the battle take place?
- When did it take place?
- Why did it take place where it did?
- How did the battle turn out?

2. Each partnership should share the information about its specific chapter with its teammates, so that each team is knowledgeable about both chapters.

3. Circulate and Monitor   Visit each team to make sure partners locate the information they need for their reading guides and are staying on task. You may need to circulate again to make sure that students are sharing accurate and complete information and that they are gaining an understanding of the chapter they did not read.

4. Use **Numbered Heads** for teams to share answers from their reading guides. Continue this discussion until all of the important points from each chapter have been brought out.

SUMMARIZING PART 4

Part 4 Check-Up   Use Check-Up 4 (TG page 105) to assess learning in Part 4.

ALTERNATE ASSESSMENT
Ask students to write a script for a political commentator to deliver on the television news that answers one of the following questions, which link the big ideas across chapters.

1. Making Connections   What was the background for each of the three goals the delegates wanted to accomplish in the Declaration of Independence? (Good government: *Belief in the rights of Englishmen and resentment of oppressive actions taken by English government;* Wrongs: *Examples of oppressive British actions;* Independence: *Realization that no compromise was possible with Britain.*)

2. Making Connections   What advantages should be chalked up to, first, the British and, second, the American sides in August 1776? *(The British were stronger financially and militarily, but the Americans had their common ideals and the advantage of fighting on their home ground.)*

USING THE RUBRICS

To assess these writing assignments, group projects, and activities, scoring rubrics have been provided at the back of this Teaching Guide. Be sure to explain the rubrics to your students.

DEBATING THE ISSUE
Use the topic below to stimulate debate.

Resolved   That the American Revolution was inevitable. (To add interest to the debate, you might have some students take the parts of firebrands such as Thomas Paine and Patrick Henry, who felt war must come. Other students should speak for John Dickinson and Joseph Hewes, who felt there was room for freedom within the British empire.

MAKING ETHICAL JUDGMENTS
The following activities ask students to consider issues of ethics.

1. To appreciate the difficult issues surrounding independence, write a dialogue in which William and Benjamin Franklin explain their different decisions regarding independence. To understand William's feeling and opinions, do additional research on the Loyalists and their support of their mother country in the war.

2. The author poses a number of questions regarding decisions by Jefferson, Adams, and other delegates on the issue of slavery. Why do you think they believed that creating a Union was more important at that time than the issue of slavery? (Students should review the points made in the text and do further research if possible.)

PROJECTS AND ACTIVITIES

Reading the Declaration of Independence   Depending on the level of your students, either read aloud or ask students to read aloud the entire Declaration, found on pages 190-192. Highlight and discuss significant portions. You might also want to ask a group of students to review the 27 grievances against King George listed on pages 191-192. Ask them to translate the list into modern English and present it to the class.

Writing Rhymes   Read aloud the following lines written about Washington and the Continental army:

> *Huzzah, huzzah, to Washington and his band*
> *With their brave help we'll have freedom in our land.*

Then ask small groups of students to write and recite rhymes that identify or say something about various figures they have read about in Part 4.

Reenacting History   Students can choose to personify each of the delegates named in Chapter 16. (If time allows, you might have students research additional delegates in the school or community library.) Conduct a mock opening session of Congress in which each member introduces himself.

Biography   Who was Benjamin Banneker and why did Thomas Jefferson write to him? Have students research and report on the life of this fascinating American.

Political Cartoons   Refer students to the political cartoon on page 88. Ask students to point out details that the cartoonist used to poke fun at the Edenton Patriots. *(Students might note the unflattering facial features or clothing styles, the unattended child, the chaos, and so on.)* Next, challenge students to draw a political cartoon of what became known as the Edenton Tea Party from the Patriot point of view. Post these cartoons on the bulletin board.

A Storytelling Bee   Using the chronologies on pages 85 and 202, help students compile a list of the main events leading to the adoption of the Declaration of Independence. Have students organize a storytelling circle and create a tale called "Path to Independence." The story might begin with such lines as "In 1775, delegates traveled from near and far to attend a special meeting in Philadelphia. Everyone knew that trouble was brewing." Ask each student in the circle to add a new part to the story. If possible, record the "story bee" so that students can listen to their oral tale.

LOOKING AHEAD

Expressing Opinions

Tell students that in 1776, John Adams remarked:

> *There will be no end to it [talk of independence]. New claims will arise; women will demand a vote; lads from twelve to twenty-one will not think their rights enough attended to; and every man who has not a farthing [1/4 penny], will demand an equal voice with any other, in all acts of state.*

Do students think Adams was correct? Why or why not? (Encourage students to refer to the principles in the Declaration of Independence.) Next, have students write letters in which either Abigail Adams or Benjamin Banneker expresses an opinion about the Declaration. Save these letters to compare with the reaction of women and African Americans as described in Part 5.

PART 5 FIGHTING THE WAR

CHAPTERS 22–28

THE BIG IDEAS

While General Henry Knox fought redcoats, his wife Lucy managed the family's business and finances. In a 1777 letter to her husband, Lucy revealed a new independent spirit:

I hope that when you come home from war you will not consider yourself as commander in chief of your house—but be convinced…that there is now such a thing as equal command.

Lucy's words reflected the changes in America. Freedom was in the air—and everyone wanted to breathe it. The war effort involved men and women, young and old, whites and blacks. Part 5 tells the story of the "people's war" for independence.

INTRODUCING PART 5

SETTING GOALS

Write the Part title on the board. Ask students what goes into fighting a war. Brainstorm a list of people who are involved. What does each one do? Help students see that the effort to win a major war involves more than just military action.

To set goals for Part 5, tell students that they will
• identify groups and individuals involved in the Revolution.
• describe the Patriots' major setbacks and triumphs.
• explain the turning point of the war.

SETTING THE CONTEXT FOR READING

Thinking About the Big Ideas   You might write this proverb from *Poor Richard's Almanack* on the board: "Little strokes fell great oaks." Ask: Why might this be good advice for the Patriots? Put up a sheet of poster board on the bulletin board entitled *Little Strokes That Won the War*. As students read, have them enter examples of the Patriots chipping away.

Making Predictions   Although the Americans had had successes at Bunker Hill, Sullivan's Island, and Great Bridge, the war was just getting started. The British still had the most feared army and most powerful navy, and their empire stretched around the world. Have students make predictions about what the Americans would have to do, what the British might do, who might help the Americans, and so on. Students can list their predictions in their notebooks, and check them as they read.

SETTING A CONTEXT IN SPACE AND TIME

Revolutionary War Room Map Activity   If you have not yet begun the Revolutionary War Room map described on TG page 24. Have students locate and mark:

Breed's and Bunker Hills (Boston)	42°15'N 71°00'W
Sullivan's Island (Charleston, SC)	32°52'N 80°00'W

Using a Time Line   Explain that all the events in this Part took place in a two-year period. How can they be shown on the class time line? Discuss how to link a micro-time line to the large one.

1 Class Period   Homework: Student Study Guide p. 31

Chapter Summary
Women helped write the story of the Revolution. They served on the home front and the battlefront. The experience left many American women thirsting for greater equality.

Key Vocabulary
hardtack   blockade

1. CONNECT

Continue with the idea that the American Revolution was a "people's war," one that involved all the people. Suggest that students make a three-column list with the headings *Men, Women,* and *Children.* As they read the chapter, encourage them to list various jobs that each group did to support the war effort.

2. UNDERSTAND

1. Read pages 106-107. Discuss: How do the women described in these pages reinforce the British officer's statement that "We should have enough to do to conquer the women." *(They proved that American women were willing to fight for the cause.)*
2. Read the rest of the chapter. Discuss: What are some ways that women and children contributed to the war effort? *(Women ran farms and businesses, sewed clothes for soldiers, made gunpowder and cannonballs, cared for the wounded, did the army's laundry. Children made cartridges, carried bullets, sewed soldiers' bags, and baked biscuits for the army.)*

3. CHECK UNDERSTANDING

Writing   Invite students to imagine that they are young Patriots during the American Revolution. Ask them to write a journal entry describing what they and their mothers did for the war effort one day.

Thinking About the Chapter (Evaluating)   Encourage students to evaluate whether the Patriots would have succeeded without the help of their women and children.

MORE ABOUT...
Women in the Revolution
One favorite story about Molly Pitcher was that, as she stretched her legs apart to brace herself before ramming a cannonball into a cannon, a British cannonball sailed right between them. Though it ripped away part of her petticoats, she was otherwise unharmed and went right on with her work. Following the war, the Pennsylvania Assembly awarded her a pension of $40 a year for her war service.

Another woman who distinguished herself in the Revolution was 16-year-old Sybil Luddington. On the night of April 26, 1777, a messenger rode up to inform her father, who was a colonel of the local militia, that an attack was about to take place on Patriot munitions stored at Danbury, Connecticut. The messenger and his horse were too exhausted to carry the alarm further, so Sybil volunteered. She rode 40 miles that night, spreading the alarm to the surrounding militia.

HISTORY ARCHIVES
A History of US Sourcebook
#15, From Abigail Adams, *Letter to John Adams* (1776)

NOTE FROM THE AUTHOR
Historian/educator Paul Gagnon says a proper history text should provide "lively chronological narrative and regular pauses in that narrative, to look in depth at particular people, events, ideas, and turning points. Neither alone is enough. Students need the large story over time to see the place and significance of topics selected for study in depth." I agree.

ACTIVITIES/JOHNS HOPKINS TEAM LEARNING
See the Student Team Learning Activity on TG page 74. This activity should be completed before reading Chapters 23 and 25.

MEETING INDIVIDUAL NEEDS

James Forten lived an adventurous and successful life. Visual learners might benefit by illustrating events in his life. Assign events to different students to illustrate. Together, students can assemble the illustrations into a comic book entitled *The Life and Times of James Forten*.

LINKING DISCIPLINES

History/Math

Use the figures for African Americans in Revolutionary America given in Thinking About the Chapter (500,000 in the South; 50,000 in the other colonies) to pose two math problems to the class: (1) How many times more African Americans were living in the South than in the other states? *(500,000 divided by 50,000 equals 10 times as many in the South)* (2) What fraction of African Americans were living in the South, and what fraction were living in the North? *(500,000 divided by 550,000 equals 10/11 living in the South; 50,000 divided by 550,000 equals 1/11 in the North)*

CHAPTER 23

FREEDOM FIGHTERS

PAGES 110–115

1 Class Period   Homework: Student Study Guide p. 32

Chapter Summary

Perhaps nobody understood the limits on equality better than people of African ancestry. Some seized offers of freedom from the British. Others fought to plant the seeds of racial freedom in their own land.

Key Vocabulary

privateer   powder boy (monkey)   pueblo

1. CONNECT

Open the chapter study by asking students if all African Americans were enslaved at the time of the American Revolution. Help them see that though the majority were enslaved, there were many who were free, working as artisans, farmers, servants, sailors, and laborers.

2. UNDERSTAND

1. Read pages 110-112. Discuss: If you had been an African American living in Philadelphia during the Revolution, do you think you would have supported the Patriots or the British? Why? *(Encourage students to think in terms of who promised more, who might be trusted more, and whose ideals were more appealing.)*

2. Read page 113. Discuss: Why was equality a radical idea in the 1770s? *(Most people believed social stability depended on people "knowing their place" rather than everyone being on the same level.)*

3. Read pages 114-115. What was happening in New Spain during the first years of the American Revolution? *(Francisco Atanasio Dominguez, a Franciscan missionary from Mexico, led an expedition to find a route from Santa Fe, New Mexico to Monterey, California.)* Have students trace the route of the expedition on a large map.

3. CHECK UNDERSTANDING

Writing   Ask students to write a one-paragraph biographical sketch of James Forten.

Thinking About the Chapter (Making Inferences)   Let the class know that during the Revolution, about 500,000 African Americans were living in the South and 50,000 in the North. Most of them were living in slavery. Have students infer why Southerners were more reluctant to accept African Americans as soldiers than were people from the other states.

1 Class Period   **Homework: Student Study Guide p. 33**

Chapter Summary

The cause of liberty drew people from many nations and religions into the conflict. They contributed leadership, money, and, in some cases, their lives.

Key Vocabulary

marquis   drillmaster   recruits   dragoon

1. CONNECT

Remind students of the mixed ancestry of the American colonists and ask them to name some of the places they came from. Refer them to the chapter title, and invite them to draw inferences about what it portends.

2. UNDERSTAND

1. Read pages 116-117. Discuss: Why did soldiers from other countries come to take part in the Revolution? (*Some came because peace had put them out of work in Europe. Others came because they believed in the cause of liberty.*)
2. Read the rest of the chapter. Discuss: What effects did Lafayette and von Steuben have on the Continental army? (*Lafayette brought his own troops and money, and became a highly regarded general on Washington's staff. Von Steuben was a drillmaster that made the American army as well-trained as the British army.*) How did the contributions of Haym Salomon match the sacrifices of the soldiers on the battlefield? (*To help finance the American war effort, Salomon gave the nation nearly everything he owned. He also spied on the British in New York and was captured and imprisoned twice by them.*)

3. CHECK UNDERSTANDING

Writing   Ask students to write a one-paragraph biographical sketch of one of the following: Marquis de Lafayette, Baron Friedrich von Steuben, Haym Salomon, Robert Morris.

Thinking About the Chapter (Making Inferences)   Encourage students to use this chapter and their own knowledge of human behavior to discuss how something as terrible as war can bring out the best and the worst in people. (*Students should recognize that although there is cruelty and killing in war, the participants also show self-sacrifice and dedication to a higher cause.*)

READING NONFICTION

Analyzing Rhetorical Devices

Refer students to Jefferson's words to the Native Americans on page 119. Discuss that an important part of persuasive speaking is using language and images the audience understands. Ask partners to analyze Jefferson's explanation for words and phrases that will make his audience of Indians understand and support his argument. (*little island beyond the great water, young and weak, say we were their slaves, were determined to be free*)

MORE ABOUT...

Robert Morris

Robert Morris was a successful financier through most of his life, much to the benefit of the Patriots. But in his later years, he would not be so lucky. In the 1790s, he lost so much money speculating on western land sales that he was sent to debtor's prison in Philadelphia for three years. One of his visitors was George Washington, who dined with the prisoner in his "hotel with grated doors."

LINKING DISCIPLINES

History/Literature

Call on students to compare the beginning of the poem about Jack Jouett's ride on page 120 with the beginning of Longfellow's poem on page 69. What similarities can they discover? (*Students should recognize the driving beat in both as well as the similar lines "Hardly anyone has heard of the ride" in the Jouett poem and "Hardly a man is now alive" in Longfellow's poem.*)

MORE ABOUT...

American Loyalties

During the American Revolution, it is estimated that Americans fell into three groups—one-third Patriots, one-third Loyalists, and one-third on neither side. You may want to have students consider how each group would be affected by Lord Dunmore's proclamation.

GEOGRAPHY CONNECTIONS

On a large map of Africa, have students locate Ethiopia. Let them know that while the majority of Africans brought to the United States were from West Africa, at that time *Ethiopian* was a term often used to refer to any black people. The use of this name for them dated back to the days of ancient Greece.

LINKING DISCIPLINES

History/Drama

Invite a volunteer group to take the incident of Thomas Marshall's servant fooling the British and write it up as a short skit. Encourage them to show the characteristics the servant must have had (courage, intelligence, wit) and to make up other characters with whom he might have dealt (Thomas Marshall, Colonel Woodford, British officers, American soldiers). Ask them to cast and perform it for the class.

GEOGRAPHY CONNECTIONS

Revolutionary War Room Map Activity

Have students continue the Revolutionary War Room map described on TG page 24. Have them locate and mark:

Great Bridge	36°37'N	76°07'W
Williamsburg	37°15'N	76°37'W
Norfolk	36°52'N	76°15'W

1 Class Period   Homework: Student Study Guide p. 33

Chapter Summary

Virginians are forced to choose to rebel or to support the king when their royal governor proclaims "all indentured servants, Negroes, and others…free" if they are willing and able to defend the Crown.

Key Vocabulary

regulars

1. CONNECT

Have students recount the dilemma that many African Americans faced (Chapter 23) in choosing sides in the American Revolution. *(joining the British in hopes of being granted freedom or joining the Patriots to fight for the ideals of liberty)*

2. UNDERSTAND

1. Read the chapter. Discuss: How does Lord Dunmore's proclamation intensify the dilemma for African Americans? How does it make life more difficult there for both whites and blacks? *(Students should recognize the various points of the dilemma—possible freedom vs. Rebel ideals for the blacks, loss of property for whites, being forced to take one side or the other with no middle ground possible.)* What clue do you have that Lord Dunmore was not sincere in his offer to Virginia's slaves? *(Dunmore did not free his own slaves.)*
2. Discuss: Why can deception be as powerful a weapon of war as armies and guns? *(Students should recognize the value of good intelligence and canniness in using it in war.)* How does what happened to Norfolk show that the Revolution was not simply Americans against British? *(Both sides had a hand in burning Norfolk, each for their own reasons. American Patriots were fighting American Loyalists, too.)*

3. CHECK UNDERSTANDING

Writing   Ask students to create a two-column chart in their notebooks with the headings *Great Bridge* and *Bunker Hill*. Have them write sentences of comparison for the two battles.

Thinking About the Chapter (Making Inferences)   The author wants to know why Lord Dunmore would seize a Rebel printing press. Encourage students to suggest answers. *(Responses should include denying the Rebels a press on which to produce propaganda against the British, or to publish accounts of the battle so the rest of the Americans could learn about it.)*

CHAPTER 26 FIGHTING A WAR

1 Class Period   Homework: Student Study Guide p. 34

Chapter Summary

The opening battles of the war went badly for Washington. His strategy rested less on pursuing victory and more on avoiding capture.

Key Vocabulary

retreat   Hessians   mercenaries

1. CONNECT

Ask students what advertisements they have seen that attempt to get people to join the military services. What is offered? What promises are made? Let them know that this chapter will reveal the problems of getting people to join the Continental army.

2. UNDERSTAND

1. Read pages 123-124 up to "The British didn't just sit around...." Discuss: What challenges faced the leaders of the Patriot army at the beginning of the Revolution? (*Congress had no money to pay the troops, who had to supply their own clothes and guns. Some of the soldiers deserted. Others stayed for only three months.*)
2. Read the rest of the chapter. Discuss: What traits do you think Washington demonstrated during the disastrous early months of the war? Why were they crucial to the new nation? (*His leadership inspired most of the troops to stay. He kept cool in battle. He knew when to retreat to save his army.*)

3. CHECK UNDERSTANDING

Writing Have students imagine they are young soldiers in Washington's army. Have them write a letter home describing what happened to them at the Battle of Long Island, and how they feel about Washington and their chances in the war.

Thinking About the Chapter (Evaluating) Encourage the class to evaluate the military ability and prospects of the new American nation in the war's early days. What will the Continental army need to be able to win the war? (*Possible response: The army's abilities and prospects were quite low at the start of the war. Students should recognize that the army would need better training, more arms and uniforms, regular pay, longer enlistments, and perhaps help from other countries.*)

READING NONFICTION

Analyzing Point of View

Refer students to the first two paragraphs of the chapter. Ask students to identify Hakim's attitude toward the reader's role in learning American history, and how they can tell. (*Hakim seems to be saying that she is hoping the text will give readers enough interest to research the subject more fully themselves: "Of course, you can read about them on your own."*)

GEOGRAPHY CONNECTIONS

Revolutionary War Room Map Activity

Have students continue the Revolutionary War Room map described on TG page 24. Explain that after the British abandoned Boston in March 1776, Washington and his army moved from Boston down to the New York City area, many of them traveling on foot and dragging cannon with them. Encourage them to trace a path they might have taken to New York and to make a rough estimate of the distance they traveled.

Boston	42°15'N	71°00'W
Long Island		
East River		

MORE ABOUT...

Hessians

In the 1700s, Hesse was an independent province ruled by a royal family in what is today Germany. To make money, these rulers hired out their army to the highest bidder. While the soldiers themselves received some pay, their ruler took a large cut of their rental from, in the case of the American Revolution, Britain.

READING NONFICTION

Analyzing Text Organization

Have students identify the text organization of this chapter. (*sequence or chronological order*) Ask students to discuss why the author chose this method to present her information. (*to help readers understand the sequence of events leading up to the surrender of Burgoyne at Saratoga, an important victory for the Americans*) What does the author describe after telling that Saratoga was won? (*the short and long-term effects of the victory*)

GEOGRAPHY CONNECTIONS

Use the map on page 127 to help students understand the three-pronged strategy and the role of geographic features in the battle at Saratoga.

Revolutionary War Room Map Activity

Have students continue the Revolutionary War Room map described on TG page 24. Have them locate and mark:

Saratoga	43°00'N	73°45'W
Hudson River		
Delaware River		
Lake Champlain		
Ticonderoga	43°45'N	73°22'W
Bennington	42°52'N	73°07'W

MORE ABOUT...

General Horatio Gates

Gates was born in Britain and joined the British army as a young man. He came to America to serve with the British army in the French and Indian War, and then returned home. In 1772, he retired from the army and emigrated back to America. Three years later, he entered the Continental army. His victory at Saratoga won him great praise in his new nation and, at one point, there was even talk that he might replace George Washington as commander-in-chief.

CHAPTER 27 HOW BILLY WISHED FRANCE WOULDN'T JOIN IN PAGES 126-129

1 Class Period   Homework: Student Study Guide p. 35

Chapter Summary
The American victory at Saratoga changed the war. Sensing that the Americans could win, the French jumped in on their side.

Key Vocabulary
oath of allegiance   sniper   guerrilla

1. CONNECT

Review early American setbacks in the war. Ask students to imagine what the morale of the army and other Patriots must have been like at that time. (*Morale was probably low, and many Patriots probably thought they had little chance to win.*) What positives did the Patriots have to cheer them? (*Washington's army was still in the field; they were fighting for their freedom; they were fighting to defend their homes.*)

2. UNDERSTAND

1. Read pages 126-127. What mistake in judgment did William Howe make in the winter of 1776? (*He thought the Americans were finished and could be dealt with in the spring.*) How did this reflect his background in European-style fighting? (*In Europe, armies didn't fight in the winter.*) How did Washington use this mistake to his advantage? (*He struck at British forces when they least expected it, winning small but important victories.*)
2. Read the rest of the chapter. Discuss: Why did the Americans often rely on guerrilla tactics? (*Such tactics are a way for smaller forces to beat larger and better-equipped forces.*)

3. CHECK UNDERSTANDING

Writing   Ask students to imagine that they have just fought for the Patriot side at Saratoga. Have them write a brief letter home describing the experience and their reaction to it.

Thinking About the Chapter (Drawing Conclusions)   Encourage students to discuss why Saratoga is considered a turning point in the American Revolution. How did it change British fortunes? American fortunes? (*Students may conclude that it broke British belief in inevitable victory and perhaps resolve to carry on as it strengthened American morale and gave the Patriots French money and military support so desperately needed to achieve victory.*)

28 VALLEY FORGE TO VINCENNES

PAGES 130-134

1 Class Period   Homework: Student Study Guide p. 36

Chapter Summary
The hardships of war gave Washington a battle-tested army. After Valley Forge, these troops began a campaign to sweep the British and their mercenaries off the continent.

Key Vocabulary
mutiny   quartermaster   serfs

1. CONNECT

Ask if any of the class knows what Valley Forge means in American history. If any students have visited there, ask them to recount the experience. Remind the class how ill-supplied the Patriot forces were in the early part of the war.

2. UNDERSTAND

1. Read pages 130-132. Discuss: No battles were fought at Valley Forge. So why is it considered a major American triumph? *(Soldiers drilled and trained. Their shared suffering forged a new spirit of unity and confidence. The result was a seasoned fighting force.)*
2. Read the rest of the chapter. Discuss: Why did fighting take place west of the Appalachians? *(The British encouraged Native Americans to attack American settlers. The Americans wanted to protect themselves and throw the British out of this rich region.)*

3. CHECK UNDERSTANDING

Writing   Ask students to complete a Venn diagram describing Washington's army when it arrived at Valley Forge in December 1777 and when it left Valley Forge in spring 1778.

Thinking About the Chapter (Synthesizing)   Write the following statement on the board: *The new nation was very lucky to have the leaders it did.* Engage students in a discussion of how figures they met in this chapter, and in earlier ones, support this statement.

GEOGRAPHY CONNECTIONS
Revolutionary War Room Map Activity

Have students continue the Revolutionary War Room map described on TG page 24. Have them locate and mark:

Brandywine, PA	40°00'N	75°30'W
Germantown, PA	40°00'N	75°07'W
Valley Forge	40°00'N	75°22'W
Schuylkill River		
Cahokia	38°30'N	90°07'W
Kaskaskia	37°52'N	90°00'W
Vincennes	38°37'N	87°30'W

LINKING DISCIPLINES
History/Language Arts

Ask students to read The Love of His Men feature on page 130. Then invite them to rewrite the information in the form of a "Ten Commandments for Military Officers."

MORE ABOUT...
Costs of Revolution

Resource Page 6 (TG page 114) gives students further information about the war—its costs in what part of the American population was involved in the fighting, in killed and wounded, and in monetary terms. It calls on them to do mathematical tasks using this information.

Nathan Hale

Hale had graduated from Yale in 1773 and had taught for two years before being commissioned as a lieutenant in the Connecticut militia. In 1776, he responded to Washington's request for a volunteer to spy on the British during the fighting around New York City. Posing as a schoolmaster, using his Yale diploma as a credential, he carried out his mission. As he returned to American lines, the British arrested him, having perhaps been told of his military identity and mission by Hale's cousin, who was a staunch Loyalist.

JOHNS HOPKINS TEAM LEARNING

**AFRICAN AMERICANS IN
THE AMERICAN REVOLUTION**

1 CLASS PERIOD

FOCUS ACTIVITY

1. Tell students that in this lesson they will read about freedom fighters in the American Revolution. Ask them to **Speculate** about what characteristics these freedom fighters might have. Refer them to illustrations on pages 89, 92, and 116 to get some ideas of their clothing, appearance, and age. Invite students to create a composite drawing of their speculations on the chalkboard.

2. Now refer students to illustrations of freedom fighters on pages 110, 121, and 122. Ask students to compare their speculations about a typical freedom fighter with what they see here. *(Students should mention that freedom fighters were black as well as white.)*

STUDENT TEAM LEARNING ACTIVITY/LOCATING, RECORDING, AND SHARING INFORMATION

1. Read aloud to students the story of James Forten on pages 110-112. Divide the class into teams of four students each, and have each team discuss the following questions:
* Was James Forten free or enslaved?
* What idea did he consider worth fighting for?
* What risks did he take to remain loyal to his country?
* Why was he so loyal to the American cause?

Have teams make a two-column chart titled *Who Will Give Us Freedom?* One column heading should be *Fighting for the Americans;* the other, *Fighting for the British.* Two students should Partner Read pages 112-113 in Chapter 23, the other two should Partner Read Chapter 25. As students read, they should enter the Pros and Cons for African Americans of fighting for either side. When they have finished reading, partnerships should share their information and complete their team sheets.

2. Circulate and Monitor Visit each team as students read and enter their information to answer questions and ensure that partners are on task.

3. Use **Numbered Heads** for teams to share their information with the whole class. Lead students to the understanding that good reasons for and against joining either side made the decision difficult for African Americans, especially since no one knew who would win the war.

ASSESSMENT

Part 5 Check-Up   Use Check-Up 5 (TG page 106) to assess learning in Part 5.

ALTERNATE ASSESSMENT
Ask students to write an essay answering one of the following questions, which link the big ideas across chapters.

1. Making Connections   How did the Declaration of Independence change ideas of equality in ways that the Continental Congress did not intend? *(Most delegates did not believe equality should extend to women and enslaved Africans. Even so, the Declaration inspired both groups to demand greater rights.)*

2. Making Connections   How did the spirit of rebellion extend into the conduct of the war? *(Encourage students to think of examples of how Americans refused to fight by European rules of war, but developed innovative ways to fight.)*

DEBATING THE ISSUE
Use the topic below to stimulate debate.

Resolved   That women should—and will—have a voice in government. (To provoke debate, appoint students to speak for women such as Abigail Adams, Mercy Otis Warren, and Phillis Wheatley. Other students should represent John Adams and Thomas Jefferson. You might also have Thomas Paine jump into the debate to defend women's rights.)

MAKING ETHICAL JUDGMENTS
The following activities ask students to consider issues of ethics.

1. The men who wrote the Declaration of Independence feared that true equality would tear the nation apart. Patriots such as Benjamin Rush, Benjamin Franklin, and Thomas Paine disagreed. Write a speech in which one of these figures defends a true government of the people.

2. James Forten was given an opportunity to gain his freedom by renouncing his country. Why do you think he refused? Would you have done the same thing? Explain your reasons.

PROJECTS AND ACTIVITIES
Geography of Revolution   If your class has maintained the war-room map suggested in the Part introduction, refer them to it. If not, request volunteers to draw such a map on poster board, showing major battles and dates. Ask: In which section of America did most of the major battles take place in 1776-1777: the New England states, the Middle states, or the Southern states? *(Middle states)* Why do you think the British focused on

USING THE RUBRICS

To assess these writing assignments, group projects, and activities, scoring rubrics have been provided at the back of this Teaching Guide. Be sure to explain the rubrics to your students.

this region? *(to try to split the new nation, to cut off New England from the South)*

Making Posters   You might have small groups of students design posters celebrating the contributions of women in the American Revolution. Some posters should focus on the tasks performed by everyday women, such as running family farms or businesses, making bullets, or sewing shirts for the troops. Other posters should highlight the achievements of individuals such as Mercy Otis Warren (nicknamed "Penwoman of the Revolution").

Analyzing a Quote   Read aloud the following remark made by an enslaved African, Jupitor Hammon:

> *That liberty is a great thing we know from our own feelings, and we may likewise judge so from the conduct of white people in the...war. How much money has been spent and how many lives have been lost to defend their liberty! I must say that I have hoped that...when they were so much engaged for liberty...[they might] think of the state of the blacks.*

After reflecting on Hammon's opinion of liberty and on Americans' conduct in the war, students should write a petition from Hammon requesting that Congress grant him freedom. Encourage students to include the contributions of African Americans to the Revolution.

Looking Deeper into History   Ask students to research Bernardo de Galvez. Tell them that Galvez was a Spanish official in New Orleans. He supplied some of the gunpowder that helped George Rogers Clark take Vincennes. He also sent herds of longhorns to feed Washington's hungry troops. Have students present their findings in an oral report called *Spanish Hero of the Revolution.* (Spanish-speaking students might write a tribute to Galvez in Spanish.)

Making Compromises   Tell students to draw a two-column chart on a sheet of paper. In one column, they should list facts about the American war effort before Saratoga. In the other column, have them list facts about the American war effort after Saratoga. Then challenge students to complete this sentence: *Saratoga was the turning point of the American Revolution because _____.*

Interpreting a Map   Refer students to the battle map on page 127. Tell them to imagine that they are observers for the French government. Assign students to write a report to King Louis based on the map and the caption. The report should include a description of troop movements, British blunders, and theories about the American victory. At the end of the report, students should offer reasons why France should enter the war on the side of the Americans.

LOOKING AHEAD

Making Predictions

Mention to students that while the Revolution raged, 11 of the states formed their own provisional state governments. All the political activity caused Thomas Paine to exclaim:

> *We are a people [bent] upon experiments, and though under one continental government, [we] have the happy opportunity of trying variety in order to discover the best.*

Have students predict some of the features of the new state governments, basing their predictions on their knowledge of American political ideas and ideals. Record these predictions on the chalkboard. Invite students to revise and modify this list as they work their way through Part 6.

THE BIG IDEAS

A belief in government by consent burned strongly in the hearts and minds of Americans. In 1774, a 19-year-old New Yorker named Alexander Hamilton wrote:

The only distinction between freedom and slavery consists in this: In the former state, a man is governed by laws to which he has given his consent, either in person or by his representative: In the latter, he is governed by the will of another.

A popular slogan in the 1770s put the matter more simply: "Where annual elections end, slavery begins." Even as bullets flew, Americans put their political beliefs into practice. Part 6 tells these first tentative steps in the creation of the world's first federal republic.

PART 6 EXPERIMENTS WITH INDEPENDENCE

INTRODUCING PART 6

SETTING GOALS
Write the Part title on the board. Ask: Why would experiments be needed? Help the class to see that independence and self-government were brand new ideas in the world at the time. Americans would have to look for, develop, and try new ways to put them into action.

To set goals for Part 6, tell students that they will
• explain problems in designing a balanced government.
• understand how Americans tried to safeguard their rights.
• identify the weaknesses of the Articles of Confederation.
• describe how lands west of the Appalachians became part of the new nation.

SETTING THE CONTEXT FOR READING
Thinking About the Big Ideas   Reintroduce the class to the term *constitution,* which they first encountered in Chapter 10 in connection with the Rights of Englishmen. Help them define it as a set of laws that say how a government should operate: which powers it should have over its people and which it should not. Explain that the American states were creating written constitutions, which had never been done before. Brainstorm how this change would affect government-citizen relationships. With students, list new provisions that the constitutions should contain to prevent abuses of government power. Have them keep the lists to compare with the provisions identified in Parts 6 and 7.

Drawing Conclusions About the New Nation   Elicit from students that, because of their colonial background, each American state was like a miniature country: each had its own money, army, form of government, and so on. Have students use prior knowledge to draw conclusions about how effective the Continental Congress could be in governing the new "nation."

SETTING A CONTEXT IN SPACE AND TIME

Linking Geography and Politics   Refer students to the maps on page 37, 148 and the Atlas and have them identify British, American, and Spanish territories before and after the Revolutionary War.   Have them identify the area that the Continental Congress had to make decisions for during and after the war.   If students completed the Geography Connections activity in chapter 2, have them complete the reproducible US political comparison map-they will sketch and label land claims in North America after the Treaty of Paris.   Have students compare and analyze the shift in the continental balance of power.   Invite students to speculate on the new issues Congress will have to face.

Understanding Chronology   List three dates on the chalkboard: 1781, 1783, 1784. Tell students that all three might be considered the end of the Revolutionary War. Ask them to look for details supporting each date as they read the Part. (*Battle of Yorktown; signing of Treaty of Paris; ratification of Treaty of Paris by Congress*)

29 THE STATES WRITE CONSTITUTIONS

1 Class Period　　　Homework: Student Study Guide p. 37

Chapter Summary

The principles that shaped the Constitution of the United States found their first expression in written documents produced at the state level. Two overarching concerns guided the authors' pens: protection from abuses of power and guarantees of liberty.

Key Vocabulary

separation of powers	legislative branch
executive branch	judicial branch

1. CONNECT

Pick up the earlier thread that Americans wanted government by consent of the governed. Help students see that this assumed the idea of *representative government;* that is, that citizens would exercise their consent through representatives whom they chose.

2. UNDERSTAND

1. Read pages 135-136 up to "When Americans wrote their state constitutions...." Discuss: What does *separation of powers* mean, and why did state constitutions prescribe it? *(Separation of powers means that the power in a government is divided amongst different branches of the government. The people who wrote the constitutions hoped this would keep one group from gaining too much power.)*
2. Read the rest of the chapter. Discuss: Why might you characterize the work of the state constitutional conventions as a great experiment? *(Students should note the wide variety of concerns they had to deal with, the conflicting opinions that various members held, and the tough job of trying to work out entirely new ways to govern.)*

3. CHECK UNDERSTANDING

Writing　Ask students to write a paragraph about the irony of the discussions of "freedoms" from the perspective of a woman, a Roman Catholic, or another person who was barred from voting by the early state constitutions.

Thinking About the Chapter (Making Inferences)　Encourage the class to discuss why the work of the state constitutional conventions might be useful for the nation as a whole. *(The states could act as proving grounds for ways of governing, supplying a blueprint for a national constitution.)*

READING NONFICTION

Analyzing Text Features

Call students' attention to the list of argued points for the state constitutions on page 136. Ask students why the author used this list format here. (*to summarize the main points in an easy-to-read way*)

MEETING INDIVIDUAL NEEDS

Help English language learners understand the meanings of the terms *executive branch, legislative branch,* and *judicial branch.* Have students draw the tree described on page 135, and label the three branches with their names and the offices that make them up. Then succinctly describe to students what each branch does in the government, and have them paraphrase your descriptions below each branch in the diagram.

MORE ABOUT...

George Mason

Mason's Declaration of Rights, written for Virginia and approved there in June 1776, was not only a model for other states. It had been sent to the Continental Congress immediately after its approval, and Thomas Jefferson used it for inspiration as he wrote the Declaration of Independence. Therefore, it has been said that Mason contributed more than anyone else except Jefferson to the Declaration of Independence. Mason's home, the stately mansion called Gunston Hall, with its elegant interior and lavish gardens, can still be visited today not far from Alexandria, Virginia.

READING NONFICTION

Analyzing Graphic Aids

Have students turn to the map on page 139 and consider the meaning of the symbol for a Spanish Mission. (*The cross represents the Roman Catholic Church.*) Then have them analyze whether, considering the huge expanse of New Mexico and California, there were many or few Spanish missions in the West in 1776.

GEOGRAPHY CONNECTIONS

Ask students to note the geographic distribution of the Spanish missions on the map on page 139. Ask which region had the most missions; which had the least. Discuss how rivers, mountains, and coastlines influenced the pattern of the location of missions. Have students pose and answer questions such as why missions might be clustered together. Ask them: If you had been a Spanish priest who wanted to establish a mission, what questions would you have asked about the geography of New Mexico and California?

LINKING DISCIPLINES

History/Literature

John Milton wrote his poetry during the 1600s, more than a century before the American Revolution. Yet he was widely read in colonial America by educated people. Did his words influence the Patriots? Read Milton's quote from *Areopagitica*, written in 1644, to the class. Does it remind them of anything they have heard a Patriot say?

> *Give me liberty to know, to utter, and to argue freely according to conscience above all liberties.*

GEOGRAPHY CONNECTIONS

Revolutionary War Room Map Activity

Transporting the heavy cannons from Fort Ticonderoga to the heights of Boston was truly a prodigious feat. Knox and his men had to drag them for 300 miles. Ask students to reread the paragraph describing the trek on page 140. Then on a physical map showing the region, have them identify a route they might have traveled and the kinds of terrain and rivers they would have had to cross.

CHAPTER 30 MORE ABOUT CHOICES

PAGES 138–141

1 Class Period   Homework: Student Study Guide p. 38

Chapter Summary

In the far West of the continent, Spanish settlers were leaving their mark on lands destined to become part of the United States. In the East, individuals such as Mary Katherine Goddard set precedents that would one day be shared by all people who called themselves American.

Key Vocabulary

artillery

1. CONNECT

On The New Nation map in the Atlas, have students locate the area of the American states (from the Atlantic Ocean to the Mississippi River). Then refer them to the American Southwest and California. Ask: What peoples live in this western area? What do you suppose their reaction is to the events in the East?

2. UNDERSTAND

1. Read pages 138-140. Discuss: Some historians say that the Revolution was also a civil war. How does the story of Lucy Knox prove this? (*The Revolution tore her family apart, dividing Patriots and Loyalists.*)
2. Map: Refer students to the map on page 139. Have them use The New Nation map in the Atlas to measure the extent of Spanish settlement in the West (distances east-west and north-south). Have them count the number of Spanish settlements in the West.
3. Read the rest of the chapter. Discuss: How does the story of Mary Katherine Goddard show that Americans still had a long way to go to fulfill their ideals? (*Students should identify the inequities reflected in her story.*)

3. CHECK UNDERSTANDING

Writing   Ask students to write a paragraph entitled *Henry Knox: How He Drove the British Out of Boston.*

Thinking About the Chapter (Making Comparisons)   Invite students to compare the contributions of Henry Knox and Mary Katherine Goddard to the war effort. What was the nature of each? Why was each necessary to success? (*Students should see that both printing presses and cannons can be critical in wartime.*)

CHAPTER 31 | WHEN IT'S OVER, SHOUT HOORAY

PAGES 142-146

1 Class Period   **Homework: Student Study Guide p. 39**

Chapter Summary
With the help of France, the Americans finally backed the British into a corner at Yorktown. The fife and drum played a tune that summed up American victory: "The World Turned Upside Down."

Key Vocabulary
stalemate

1. CONNECT

Encourage students to recap the state of the fighting in the war at the end of Chapter 28. Where will the battles move next? How will they turn out?

2. UNDERSTAND

1. Read pages 142-143 up to "Then came the most important battle of all...." Discuss: Why did the stalemate following Saratoga favor the Americans? (*It prolonged the war, caused British dissatisfaction, and gave the Americans time to strengthen themselves.*)
2. Read the rest of the chapter. Discuss: Why do you think "The World Turned Upside Down" was a fitting song for the British surrender at Yorktown? (*Students should recognize that the strongest power in the world had been defeated by one of the weakest.*)
3. After students read the margin note on page 146, ask them to explain the issues surrounding the treaty. Did the former colonies achieve their goal in fighting the war? (*Yes, the now sovereign states had gained independence and a vast territory. The treaty resolved issues of territorial claims by Britain, France, Spain, and the new United States.*)

3. CHECK UNDERSTANDING

Writing   Ask students to imagine that they are American soldiers who have just fought at Yorktown. Invite them to write a short letter home explaining what happened and how they feel.

Thinking About the Chapter (Sequencing)   Call on students to place in sequence major events from Howe's resignation in New York to the British defeat at Yorktown. Encourage them to discuss how British loss of interest, French intervention, and American training joined to America victory.

LINKING DISCIPLINES
History/Drama

The quote in the John Paul Jones feature on page 144 is one of the most famous in American history. Invite a group of volunteers to read the feature and do further research on the *Bon Homme Richard*'s battle with the *Serapis*. Ask them to write and perform a skit dramatizing the incident that sparked Jones's famous words.

MORE ABOUT...
Mad Anthony Wayne

General Anthony Wayne's nickname seems to have grown out of an exchange he had with General Washington. In 1778, Washington sent Wayne to dislodge the British from their fort at Stony Point on the Hudson River. The fort was atop a steep, rocky hill and surrounded on three sides by water and on the fourth by marshland that was flooded daily by the tide. It was thought to be impregnable. Nevertheless, when ordered to storm it, Wayne was heard to reply, "General, if you will only plan it, I'll storm hell!" On overhearing Wayne's promise, one of his men supposedly said, "The man is mad!" and the nickname was born.

GEOGRAPHY CONNECTIONS
Using Resource Page 7 (TG page 101), have students trace the course of events leading to the British surrender at Yorktown and discuss how geography helped defeat the British there.

GEOGRAPHY CONNECTIONS
Revolutionary War Room Map Activity

Have students continue the Revolutionary War Room map described on TG page 24. Have them locate and mark:

Yorktown   37°07'N   76°30'W

Turn students' attention to the cartoon on page 150, and have them point out the elements of the cartoon. Ask: What seems to be the cartoonist's point of view about what the relationship between Britain and the United States will be? (*Possible response: The cartoonist seems to be hopeful that the relationship can be peaceful, as shown by the olive branch America is holding out to Britain.*)

HISTORY ARCHIVES/
A History of US Sourcebook
#16, *Articles of Confederation* (1778)

GEOGRAPHY CONNECTIONS

On a wall map of the United States, show students the western land claims made by the various states. Virginia's claims are mentioned in the text; Massachusetts, New York, and Connecticut also claimed some of these lands. North Carolina and Georgia each claimed all the territory west to the Mississippi between their southern and northern borders. South Carolina claimed a narrow corridor of land between North Carolina and Georgia. Alternately, have students sketch the land claims made by the new states on the blank Eastern US Relief map provided in the Student Study Guide.

---

1 Class Period   Homework: Student Study Guide p. 40

Chapter Summary

When the Revolution ended, few Americans talked of the United States. Unity took the form of the loose association of states created by the Articles of Confederation. Its weaknesses paved the way for a new government—a federal republic.

Key Vocabulary

supply and demand   inflation
Articles of Confederation

1. CONNECT

Invite students to imagine a game that has no rules, where there are no set goals for winning or losing, where everyone takes any action he or she wants and agrees on nothing. Suggest that this is like the situation that the newly proclaimed United States faced.

2. UNDERSTAND

1. Read about the rocky start for the new American government on pages 147-148. Discuss: In what ways might the states have been called the Disunited States in 1781? (*They had different money, different ways of taxing, boundary squabbles, and rebellious citizens, and were independent rather than unified states.*)
2. Read the rest of the chapter. Discuss: What was the Articles of Confederation? (*the first constitution of the United States*) Why didn't it work well? (*American citizens were afraid of a strong government, so the Articles gave the national government almost no power. It could not collect taxes to pay its bills, lacked backing and participation from the states, and each state—no matter its size—had only one vote.*)

3. CHECK UNDERSTANDING

Writing   Ask students to imagine that George Washington had proclaimed himself king. Have them write a paragraph telling how the United States might be different today as a result.

Thinking About the Chapter (Making Judgments)   Engage the class in a discussion of how to balance individual liberty and reasonable government power. You might introduce the idea of social compact theory—that citizens must agree to give government certain powers so that society can operate peacefully. What powers should they give the government?

33 LOOKING NORTHWEST

PAGES 151-153

HISTORY ARCHIVES
A History of US Sourcebook
#21, *From The Northwest Ordinance* (1787)

1 Class Period   Homework: Student Study Guide p. 41

Chapter Summary
The one triumph of the national government under the Articles of Confederation was the passage of the Northwest Ordinance. This law helped ensure the orderly expansion of the United States through the admission of states on an equal footing with the rest of the nation.

Key Vocabulary
ordinance   Northwest Ordinance   township
Conestoga   involuntary servitude

1. CONNECT

Encourage students to recall what they have already learned about the movement west. Who were the pioneers? Where were they going? What were they looking for? What obstacles did they face? What was their effect on Native Americans?

2. UNDERSTAND

1. Read page 151. Discuss: What was the Northwest Ordinance and why was it another "first" for the world? *(It was an orderly plan to create new, equal states for the country, rather than keeping the territory as a colony of the United States.)*

2. Map: Refer students to the map on page 148 and have them locate the Northwest Territory on it. Make sure they understand that "northwest" referred to the territory that was northwest of the United States at that time.

3. Read the rest of the chapter. Discuss: How well would you say the Northwest Ordinance dealt with the arguing points for creation of state constitutions listed on page 136? *(Encourage students to find specific references to each of these points in this chapter. They should note that the Ordinance dealt directly with several of them.)*

3. CHECK UNDERSTANDING

Writing   Ask students to write a one-paragraph opinion of the Northwest Ordinance from the Native American point of view.

Thinking About the Chapter (Making Inferences)   Engage the class in a discussion of what Thomas Jefferson meant when he said, "If a nation expects to be ignorant and free…it expects what never was and never will be." *(Students should show an understanding that people cannot be well governed unless they know enough to make sure that their government is dealing fairly with them.)*

READING NONFICTION
Analyzing Text Organization
Have students analyze how the author wrote about the Northwest Ordinance: she generally used one paragraph to explain one aspect of the ordinance. Have students outline the parts of the ordinance by summarizing the main ideas of each paragraph in the section. (*provided a fair way for territories to become states; divided land into townships; guaranteed freedoms of Americans; called for education*)

GEOGRAPHY CONNECTIONS
Invite students to do further research on the Northwest Territory (also called the "Old Northwest") to add to the maps they made for the Geography Connections activity in Chapter 32. Their maps should show the boundaries of the states carved out of it, their names, and their dates of entry into the Union.

MORE ABOUT...
Slavery and the Northwest Ordinance
The text quotes the Northwest Ordinance: "there shall be neither slavery nor involuntary servitude in the said territory." Why did Southern slave owners agree to this prohibition? Because Congress did allow slavery in the Old Southwest—the western lands below the Ohio River.

HISTORY ARCHIVES

A History of US Sourcebook

1. #17, From Thomas Jefferson, *Notes on the State of Virginia* (1785)
2. #19, From Thomas Jefferson, *The Virginia Statute for Religious Freedom* (1786)
3. #25, George Washington, *Letter to the New Church in Baltimore*

MEETING INDIVIDUAL NEEDS

The caption on page 155 states that the main part of the second floor of Monticello was an octagon. Visual learners might benefit from drawing an eight-sided floor plan to present graphically what Jefferson did.

LINKING DISCIPLINES

History/Science

Jefferson was an avid natural scientist. He studied soils, botany, and zoology. Ask for a scientific research group to investigate this aspect of Jefferson and report their findings back to the class. (They may discover that, during his presidency, one of the tasks he assigned Lewis and Clark as they explored the Louisiana Territory was to send back biological specimens to him at the White House for his study.)

MORE ABOUT...

Pasta

Pasta may not be the only popular food that Thomas Jefferson introduced to the United States. He is also thought to have imported the knowledge of how to make ice cream from France. He was certainly one of the first to serve it at a state dinner. He served it in the middle of a crisp hot pastry, which was perhaps the nation's first ice cream sandwich. Today, Americans consume 20 pounds of ice cream per capita each year.

ACTIVITIES/JOHNS HOPKINS TEAM LEARNING

See the Student Team Learning Activity on TG page 85.

CHAPTER **34** | A MAN WITH IDEAS

PAGES 154-157

1 Class Period   Homework: Student Study Guide p. 42

Chapter Summary

Thomas Jefferson designed houses, inventions, and principles of government. The idea of separation of church and state owes its origins to Thomas Jefferson and his friend James Madison.

Key Vocabulary

intellectual   decimal system
piedmont   separation of church and state

1. CONNECT

Write *Thomas Jefferson* on the chalkboard and invite the class to tell what they have learned about him so far. Use his writing of the Declaration of Independence to help them understand that he was truly a man of ideas. Invite them to discuss why such a person would be so important in the development of a new nation.

2. UNDERSTAND

1. Read pages 154-155. Discuss: What clues to Jefferson's character can you find so far? *(Possible responses: broad interests, love of beauty, serious, cheerful, always experimenting, distrustful of slavery)*
2. Read the rest of the chapter. Discuss: Why is the Virginia Statute of Religious Freedom so important to our history? *(It gave rise to our belief in the separation of church and state, or that the state could not tell people what to believe, which was another first in world history, one that has lured countless people to the U.S. in search of religious freedom.)*

3. CHECK UNDERSTANDING

Writing   Ask students to choose the aspect of Thomas Jefferson that they most share or admire and write a paragraph describing it and telling why they chose it.

Thinking About the Chapter (Making Comparisons)   Organize the class into small groups. Using *A History of US Sourcebook*, ask the groups to read and discuss *The Virginia Statute for Religious Freedom* and *Letter to the New Church in Baltimore*. Each group should appoint someone to take notes of their discussion, paying special attention to the similarities and differences between Jefferson's and Washington's perspectives on the separation between church and state. Then each group should make a Venn diagram or other visual that clearly shows the two Founding Fathers' viewpoints.

JOHNS HOPKINS TEAM LEARNING

THOMAS JEFFERSON—STATESMAN

1 CLASS PERIOD

FOCUS ACTIVITY

1. Have students define *epitaph*. ("an inscription on a tomb or grave that commemorates or describes the person buried there") Tell them that during the 18th and 19th centuries, it was fashionable for people to write their own epitaphs as a means of evaluating their own lives.

2. Ask students to take a few minutes to write their own epitaphs, in which they include what they would like people to remember about them. Then have the class survey the epitaphs and determine which statements fall into the categories of achievement or character.

STUDENT TEAM LEARNING ACTIVITY/EVALUATING JEFFERSON'S IMPACT

1. Divide the class into teams of four students each, and have the teams review the three achievements that Jefferson wanted in his epitaph (page 156). Each team should act as a panel of judges to evaluate Jefferson's contributions and decide which one of them had the most lasting influence on the establishment and success of democracy in America. The team should consider the past, present, and possible future impact of Jefferson's contributions. The team should plan a good argument in support of its choice to present to the class.

2. Circulate and Monitor   Visit each team as the students choose Jefferson's most important contribution and construct their argument. Answer and ask questions to guide students in their work.

3. Use **Numbered Heads** for each team to share its decision and the reasons for it. Have students keep a tally for each contribution to determine which one the class as a whole feels was most influential.

4. Have students award a Founder's Prize to the most frequently chosen contribution/accomplishment. If there is no clear-cut choice, have the class consider each team's choice and its argument, and then vote to award the prize.

SUMMARIZING PART 6

Part 6 Check-Up   Use Check-Up 6 (TG page 107) to assess learning in Part 6.

ALTERNATE ASSESSMENT
Ask students to write an essay answering one of the following questions, which link the big ideas across chapters.

1. Making Connections   The states included in their constitutions some of the basic building blocks of American government. What were some of these? *(Possible responses: written constitutions, ratification of constitutions by people's representatives, separation of church and state)*

2. Making Connections   How would you compare the conflicts Americans faced during the Revolution with those they faced afterward? *(During the war: fighting the British, trying to finance the war. After the war: conflicts between the states and how governments could be designed to balance individual liberty and the government's ability to function.)*

USING THE RUBRICS

To assess these writing assignments, group projects, and activities, scoring rubrics have been provided at the back of this Teaching Guide. Be sure to explain the rubrics to your students.

DEBATING THE ISSUES
Use the topic below to stimulate debate.

Resolved   That the states should surrender as little power as possible to the central government. (Encourage "pro" students to cite past examples of abuse of power. Suggest that "con" students point out the pitfalls of government under the Articles of Confederation.)

MAKING ETHICAL JUDGMENTS
The following activities ask students to consider issues of ethics.

1. Who do you think acted in a more ethical manner: the British, who protected Native American lands west of the Appalachians, or the Americans, who designed the Northwest Ordinance for its American settlement? Why?

2. Thomas Jefferson and James Madison had to search their own consciences on the issue of state and religion. The idea that people could practice any faith—or no faith at all—was radical at the time. Write a speech in which you explain why this one freedom is the basis upon which all other freedoms rest.

PROJECTS AND ACTIVITIES
Linking Past and Present   Select interested students to locate a copy of your state constitution. Have them use this document to prepare a short oral report on the structure of your state government. In a class discussion, ask: How does the pattern of government in our state reflect ideas first developed in the 1770s? How does it differ?

In Your Own Words   Distribute copies of the following passage from the Massachusetts constitution:

The legislative department shall never exercise the executive and judicial powers, or either of them: the executive shall never exercise the legislative and judicial powers, or either of them; the judicial shall never exercise the legislative and executive powers, or either of them; to this end it may be a government of laws and not men.

Assign students to rewrite this passage, using everyday language. Encourage them to use the terms *congress/assembly, governor,* and *courts.* (You might allow students learning English to work in their primary language, translating into English when they are finished.)

Interpreting Visual Evidence   Refer students to the picture and map on pages 138 and 139. Work with the class to use details in these visuals to help brainstorm features of Spanish colonial life. To get students started, ask: What role did religion play in Spanish America? Have students write an account, based upon your discussion, of a journey along the Spanish frontier. If possible, encourage students to do additional library research.

Creative Writing   Remind students that young fifers and drummers often marched into battle with American troops. Soldiers stepped to the beat of their music and drew courage from well-known patriotic tunes. Challenge students to write a short story in which a young fifer or drummer describes the battle of Yorktown. Call on volunteers to read their stories aloud.

Reenacting History   Select volunteers to prepare a mock history lesson given by a teacher in one of the new schools in the Northwest Territory. The lesson should explain government in the territory, as well as provisions for future entry into the Union. Have one of the volunteers act as teacher for your class as a whole. When the lesson is finished, ask: What rights and responsibilities of citizenship did settlers have under the Northwest Ordinance?

Illustrated Biography   After discussing the phrase *jack-of-all-trades,* ask students to create a poster or write a short article entitled "Thomas Jefferson: America's Jack-of-All-Trades."

Designing Character Sketches   Remind students that a character sketch is a short piece of writing describing a person or type of person. It also can be a dramatic portrayal, emphasizing distinctive character traits. Have students work in teams to prepare a character sketch of Thomas Jefferson.

Word Detective   On page 146, the author mentions two Latin phrases that appear on dollar bills. Point out that another Latin phrase appears on our coins: *e pluribus unum.* Ask students to research the meaning of this term ("one out of many") and where else it appears (on the Great Seal).

LOOKING AHEAD

Interpreting a Primary Source

Tell students that in February 1787, the Continental Congress called a convention to review the Articles of Confederation. At this time, Thomas Jefferson was serving as American minister to France. When he heard the news, Jefferson declared:

This example of changing the constitution by assembling the wise men of the state, instead of assembling armies, will be worth as much to the world as all the other examples we have given it.

Ask: What do you think Jefferson meant by this remark? Lead students to understand that changing government by peaceful means, rather than by force, is yet another American "first." Tell students that the actions taken by this convention of wise men of the state forms the subject of Part 7.

THE BIG IDEAS

In 1787, Americans rolled up their sleeves and created the Constitution of the United States. The document was shaped by conflicts and the compromises that resolved them. It included imperfections born of the times. But the Constitution also gave Americans the tools for change. Poet Francis Hopkinson captured the nation's optimistic hopes for the future in a poem entitled "The New Roof: A Song for Federal Mechanics":

Come muster, my lads, your mechanical tools,
Your saws and your axes, your hammers and rules;
Bring your mallets and planes, your level and line,
And plenty of pins of American pine;
For our roof we will rise, and our song shall be,
Our government firm, and our citizens free.

The "federal mechanics" created a document that has stood the test of time. Part 7 tells how the Framers drafted a blueprint for republican government.

INTRODUCING PART 7

SETTING GOALS

Introduce Part 7 by writing *Where We Stand So Far* on the chalkboard. Invite students to create a picture of the situation in the United States in the mid-1780s, based on questions like these: What has gone right for us? What problems do we still have to face? Encourage students to assess the state of the Union, complete with troubles between the states and a weak national government.

To set goals for Part 7, tell students that they will
 • identify the major step the nation took to revamp its government.
 • describe the roles of the major figures who created the Constitution.
 • explain the major points of debate and compromises that went into creating and adopting the Constitution.

SETTING A CONTEXT FOR READING

Thinking About the Big Ideas You can lead into Part 7 by reading aloud the many questions posed by the author in the fourth paragraph on page 174. Can students meet the author's challenge to create a perfect democracy? Record students' ideas on the chalkboard, underlining areas of disagreement.

Next, write *compromise* on the chalkboard and discuss its meaning. Ask students to think about how compromise might be an essential element in bringing constructive change out of conflict. Then ask the class why compromise might be necessary to write the constitution suggested by the author. (Remind students that to be democratic, their constitution can't be a one-person document.) In a follow-up discussion, tell students that the Constitution of the United States has been called a "bundle of compromises." Based on this description, what can they guess about discussions at the Constitutional Convention of 1787? *(There were many conflicts.)*

Sequencing   Suggest to the class that they trace the major events of the Constitutional Convention by keeping notes on them in sequence. Students could keep a summary chart of the notes in their notebooks. When they have completed their notes with the final chapter, have them make a chart entitled *Steps in Creating the Constitution of the United States.* The chart might begin with "A meeting is called in Philadelphia to revamp the national government" and end with "The nation adopts the Constitution," with the other steps listed in between.

SETTING THE CONTEXT IN SPACE AND TIME
Linking Geography and Politics   Have students turn back to the map of the United States on page 148. Point out that the United States in the 1780s was already a large nation—much bigger than many European countries. Ask volunteers to recall the poor transportation and communication links at this time. You might tell students that a British traveler of the time described the nation's roads as "the most hard-hearted, wicked roads on earth."

Next, explore why strong state governments might benefit the nation in the 1780s. *(They could administer some laws to help society to operate within their borders.)* Then have students consider some of the drawbacks of strong state governments. *(They might be in conflict with one another or be jealous of one another, which might promote disunity.)* Ask students to imagine that it is 1787. They are part of a committee appointed to draw up new ways to govern the nation. What tasks should be assigned to the states? What tasks should *not* be assigned to the states? Encourage students to review their ideas as they work through Part 7.

Using a Time Line   Point out to the class that you are about to study the last Part of Book Three, and ask them to use class and individual time lines to review the journey they have made as time travelers from the trial of Peter Zenger in 1735. Tell them that they will end this part of their journey in 1791, when the rights defended at Zenger's trial were guaranteed to all Americans.

MORE ABOUT...

Minister Jefferson

Although Jefferson went to France to replace Franklin, the modest Jefferson had a different take on this assignment. When he presented himself to the French minister for foreign affairs in Paris in 1785, the minister inquired, "You replace Monsieur Franklin?" Jefferson replied, "I succeed him. No one can replace him." When Jefferson learned the names of the delegates chosen to make up the Constitutional Convention, he was so impressed with them that he called the group "really an assembly of demigods."

MEETING INDIVIDUAL NEEDS

Some students may wish to discover why none of the firebrands of the Revolution—Samuel Adams, Patrick Henry, or Thomas Paine—were delegates to the Constitutional Convention. Ask researchers to find out what happened to each of them and why they were no longer intimately involved with national affairs. Have the researchers present their findings to the class.

LINKING DISCIPLINES

History/Science

The Royal Society is one of the oldest ongoing associations in the world. It was founded in 1660 as the Royal Society of London for Improving Natural Knowledge. It also ranks as the foremost scientific organization in the world. Ask students to research its aims, how one becomes a member, and its accomplishments, and prepare written reports of their findings.

CHAPTER 35 A PHILADELPHIA WELCOME

PAGES 158–161

1 Class Period   Homework: Student Study Guide p. 43

Chapter Summary

Led by James Madison, the Virginians traveled to the Constitutional Convention armed with ideas for change. Instead of revising the Articles of Confederation, delegates found themselves debating a new proposal, the so-called Virginia Plan.

Key Vocabulary

Constitutional Convention   Virginia Plan

1. CONNECT

Ask students to name prominent leaders of the American Revolution and list them on the chalkboard. Why might they be expected to play a role in the Constitutional Convention? Explain that some of these leaders would be absent. Thomas Jefferson was in France, John Adams was in Britain, and Patrick Henry refused to come.

2. UNDERSTAND

1. Read page 158. Discuss: Why do you think Philadelphia was chosen as the site of the Constitutional Convention? *(Students should note its central location, its history for holding such meetings, and its size.)*
2. Read the rest of the chapter. Discuss: What talents did James Madison bring to the Constitutional Convention? *(He was hard-working, well-educated, and well-prepared, had a knowledge of government, and had not only helped write Virginia's constitution, but helped produce the Virginia Plan of government that the Constitutional Convention used as its base.)*

3. CHECK UNDERSTANDING

Writing   Ask students to imagine they are James Madison. Have them write a persuasive letter to one of the other leaders of the time about why the Articles of Confederation should be scrapped, not revised.

Thinking About the Chapter (Recognizing Point of View)
Help students recognize that the work of the Constitutional Convention was radically changed in midstream. Ask: What was the point of view of many delegates toward their job when they came to Philadelphia? How did Madison's point of view differ? *(Many delegates came just to revise the Articles of Confederation; Madison came to throw them out and start over.)*

1 Class Period   Homework: Student Study Guide p. 43

Chapter Summary

In public, delegates eagerly enjoyed the charms of Philadelphia. Meanwhile, ordinary Philadelphians knew nothing of the bitter conflicts taking place each day behind the locked doors of the Pennsylvania State House.

Key Vocabulary

median   Framers

1. CONNECT

On the chalkboard, write *All the Comforts of Home.* Ask students: What do you think this means to Americans today? Encourage students to list the ideals: indoor plumbing, electricity, comfortable bedrooms, privacy, heating and air conditioning, well-equipped kitchens, and so on. Invite students to contrast all this to the living conditions of the Constitutional Convention delegates, which they will now read about.

2. UNDERSTAND

1. Read pages 162-164 up to "It was a good thing...." Discuss: How do the living conditions make the delegates to the Constitutional Convention all the more admirable? *(Students should recognize the sacrifices they had to make and the discomfort they endured while having to act reasonably and patiently.)*

2. Read the rest of the chapter. Discuss: Why did the delegates choose to operate in secrecy? *(to avoid public conflict before they finalized their ideas; to be able to offer ideas freely and debate them freely; to be able to change their minds without being seen publicly to back down)* How would you compare life in 1787 with life now? Have students make comparisons of sanitation, size of cities, age of population, health, and common practices of the people.

3. CHECK UNDERSTANDING

Writing   Ask students to imagine that they are delegates to the Constitutional Convention. Have them write a brief letter home reporting an experience they have had.

Thinking About the Chapter (Making Judgments)   Ask: Are the reasons offered for secrecy at the convention good enough for you? Encourage students to offer reasons why governmental secrecy can be bad as well as good. Invite them make two lists— for and against secrecy—and judge which outweighs the other.

READING NONFICTION

Analyzing Point of View

Refer the class to Sense Being Preferable to Sound (page 171). What was Franklin's point of view about the town's request? (*They should save money by not building the steeple, and use Franklin's gift to start a library so the residents might be educated.*) How does his reply illustrate Franklin's approach to life? (*Possible response: Throughout his life, Franklin was interested in education, inquiry, and democracy. His reply shows he wanted other people to feel the same way he did.*)

MORE ABOUT...

Famous Debtor

Robert Morris was one Framer who spent time in debtor's prison. (See Chapter 24.) Another who was threatened with that fate was James Wilson, who in 1797, lost a great deal of money in land speculation. To avoid being imprisoned in Pennsylvania, he fled to North Carolina. (He was an associate justice of the Supreme Court at the time.) He died the following year.

MEETING INDIVIDUAL NEEDS

To reinforce how the federal system works, call on volunteers to come to the front of the room. Divide them into central government and state government groups. Then have the groups alternate naming the powers of their government stated in the text.

ACTIVITIES/JOHNS HOPKINS TEAM LEARNING

See the Student Team Learning Activity on TG page 98. Students should complete this activity before reading Chapter 38.

---

1 Class Period   Homework: Student Study Guide p. 44

Chapter Summary

Many issues divided delegates, but the most explosive one was of power. Some delegates wanted strong state governments; others wanted a strong national government. Out of the debate came a compromise: a federal system with shared power.

Key Vocabulary

confederation   federation   federal   federalism

1. CONNECT

Ask the class to construct a cast of characters for the Constitutional Convention in their notebooks. Have them jot down names and brief descriptions of the important personalities identified in the past three chapters. Invite them to continue the list as they work through this chapter.

2. UNDERSTAND

1. Read about the Framers described on pages 167-171, and have students enter them on their cast lists. Discuss each person: Why do you think this man will be an important voice at the convention?

2. On page 169, the author writes that democracy meant something different in the 18th century than it does today. Ask: How might democracy have a "different ring" in different eras? (*Many more types of people can vote now than in the 18th century; more freedoms are protected now.*)

3. Read the rest of page 171. Discuss: What is the difference between a confederation and a federation? Why do you think the convention chose a federation? (*Confederation: government of partners who each keep all important power for themselves. Federation: government that divides power between central and state governments. The convention probably chose a federation because a confederation had not worked.*)

3. CHECK UNDERSTANDING

Writing   Ask students to write a one-paragraph biography of one of the convention cast.

Thinking About the Chapter (Making Comparisons)   Review separation of powers (page 135). Ask: How does the federal system reflect another type of separation of powers? (*between central and state governments*) Why did the delegates choose it as a compromise? (*It is another way to limit and balance power.*)

---

38 ROGER TO THE RESCUE

PAGES 172-173

1 Class Period   **Homework: Student Study Guide p. 45**

Chapter Summary

Another conflict over power erupted when big and little states battled over representation. Roger Sherman settled the matter with a compromise that created a bicameral legislature.

Key Vocabulary

Three-Fifths Compromise   Virginia Plan
New Jersey Plan   Great Compromise
Connecticut Plan

1. CONNECT

Remind students that the Constitution has been called a "bundle of compromises." Tell students this chapter deals with another compromise about power. Have students enter Roger Sherman in their cast of characters.

2. UNDERSTAND

1. Read the chapter. Discuss: How did the Virginia and New Jersey plans pit large states against small states? *(The Virginia Plan based representation in the legislative branch on population, giving large states more representatives than small states. The New Jersey Plan said all states should have the same number of representatives.)*

2. Discuss: How did the Connecticut Compromise save the Constitution? *(by dividing legislative power into two bodies and giving more populous states more representatives in the House while giving every state an equal number in the Senate)* Tell students that another name for the Connecticut Compromise is the "Great Compromise," because it was essential to the making of the Constitution.

3. CHECK UNDERSTANDING

Writing   Ask students to write a one-paragraph reply to this question: Why was a man like Roger Sherman vital to the success of the convention?

Thinking About the Chapter (Synthesizing)   Help students to see how often the Framers separated power as a way of limiting and balancing it. Ask: What do the separation of powers, the federal system, and the Connecticut Compromise all have in common? *(Possible response: They protect the rights of the small against the large, or the weak against the powerful. They limit the power that the various parts of the government have in order to limit the abuses of that power.)*

MORE ABOUT...

Convention Frustration

The wrangling that went on behind closed doors at the Constitutional Convention during the hot summer of 1787 seemed endless. At one point, it even got to the steady president, George Washington. "I almost despair," he wrote. "The men who oppose a strong & energetic government are, in my opinion, narrow minded politicians, or are under the influence of local views."

JUST WHAT IS A CONSTITUTION?

PAGES 174-177

READING NONFICTION

Analyzing Graphic Aids

Have students study the painting of the United States' official seal on page 174. Ask them to identify the symbols it uses. (*eagle, olive branch, sheaf of arrows*) Ask: What do these symbols represent? (*The eagle stands for bravery, intelligence, and power. The olive branch stands for peace. The sheaf of arrows stands for military preparedness.*) Have students explain how these symbols relate to the United States.

MORE ABOUT...

The English Bill of Rights

The document that set out the rights and liberties of the people of England following the Glorious Revolution had a profound effect on the U.S. Constitution. Some of the rights found in both documents include prohibitions on excessive bail and the right to jury trial. The clause in the English Bill of Rights prohibiting excessive bail and cruel and unusual punishments was used, almost word for word, in Amendment Eight of the U.S. Constitution.

HISTORY ARCHIVES

A History of US Sourcebook

#20, The Constitution of the United States (1787)

1 Class Period   **Homework: Student Study Guide p. 45**

Chapter Summary

The Framers intended the Constitution to be the supreme law of the land. Their gift to future generations was a provision for amendment so that the document could change with the times.

Key Vocabulary

checks and balances   supreme law
amendments   ratify

1. CONNECT

Call on students to identify and review the provisions of the Constitution they have learned about so far. Let them know that in this chapter, they will recap these provisions and learn about a few more—and why the Constitution still works.

2. UNDERSTAND

1. Read pages 174-175. Discuss: Why did the Framers build a system of checks and balances into the Constitution? (*To protect individual liberty, the power to govern must be limited, and having one branch check another is a means to limit power.*

2. Read the rest of the chapter. Discuss: What were two basic aims of the Constitutional Convention and how well did the Constitution reach them? (*For government by the consent of the governed, it provides for elected representatives. For guarantee of basic rights, consult the Bill of Rights on page 199.*)

3. Turn students' attention to Three-Fifths of a Person (page 174). Have students speculate why great people sometimes allow bad practices to continue. (*Possible response: The delegates were concerned with the task of creating a new government, which required them to compromise on issues that would ordinarily be very important to them.*)

3. CHECK UNDERSTANDING

Writing   Ask students to use a graphic organizer to create a comparison of powers granted to state and federal governments at the time of the ratification of the Constitution. Have them pick one power from the list and write a one-paragraph explanation about it.

Thinking About the Chapter (Drawing Conclusions)   Invite students to describe the amendment process. Then engage students in a discussion of why it is absolutely crucial to maintaining the Constitution as the supreme law of the land over the centuries. (*Time not only begets change but also can demand it. Therefore, the flexibility to change must be available.*)

40 GOOD WORDS AND BAD

1 Class Period　　　**Homework: Student Study Guide p. 46**

Chapter Summary
The Constitution contains flaws, especially the provisions dealing with slavery. But the words *We the People* held out an idea for perfection. Through the amendment process, Americans have reached for that ideal.

Key Vocabulary
preamble　　　slave trade　　　cotton gin

1. CONNECT

Ask the class to explain how the Constitutional Convention dealt with how the enslaved Africans were to be counted in the new nation. *(Each would count as three-fifths of a person.)* What other provisions would the Constitution make regarding slavery? How did it deal with other groups—women and Native Americans? Why? Invite students to read this chapter to find out.

2. UNDERSTAND

1. Read the chapter. Discuss: How is the concept of *We the People* different today from what it was in 1787? *(Possible response: Democracy has continually broadened to include more and more of the nation's citizenry.)* How did the issue of slavery force the Framers to choose between principles and practicality? *(Possible response: The South refused to give up slavery, and the North had to accept it for practical political reasons—gaining national unity.)*
2. Resource Page 8 (TG page 116) calls for students to rewrite four grievances against King George III from the Declaration and then to tell how certain provisions in the Constitution sought to remedy these grievances in the new American government.

3. CHECK UNDERSTANDING

Writing　Ask students to think about what change or addition they might like to make in the Constitution. Have them write out their amendments and then discuss them in class.

Thinking About the Chapter (Comparing Points of View)
What was paradoxical about the points of view of Rutledge, Mason, and Jefferson on slavery? *(Rutledge fought to maintain slavery, yet freed his own slaves. Mason and Jefferson both opposed slavery yet did not free their slaves.)* Challenge students to speculate on the reasons for these paradoxes.

CHAPTER 41

NO MORE SECRETS

LINKING DISCIPLINES

History/Art

Refer the class to the two illustrations on page 183 of Washington's chair. Invite students to create color drawings of what that sun might look like.

MORE ABOUT...

Alexander Hamilton

Although Patrick Henry believed that the Constitutional Convention would make the central government too powerful, Alexander Hamilton felt just the opposite. A proponent of a still stronger central government, he called the Constitution a "shilly-shally thing of milk and water which could not last." Nevertheless, Hamilton became one of the major proponents for ratification of the Constitution.

1 Class Period   Homework: Student Study Guide p. 47

Chapter Summary

Each delegate had reservations about the Constitution, but few believed any better plan could be devised. They turned the plan over to the states for ratification, triggering yet another round of conflict and debate.

Key Vocabulary

ratification

1. CONNECT

Help students recapture the hot summer in Philadelphia: the issues the Constitutional Convention had to deal with, the wrangling, and the secrecy. Point out that now the Constitution has been written and the convention is drawing to a close. Is all the wrangling over?

2. UNDERSTAND

1. Read the chapter. Discuss: What "miracle" did Washington write to Lafayette about? *(that the delegates united to form a national government)* Why was it miraculous to him? *(Possible response: It wasn't always certain whether the convention would be able to complete its work.)*
2. Discuss: For what reasons did delegates and non-delegates object to ratification of the Constitution? *(not good enough, too much power to the central government and too little to the states, no immediate end to slavery and the slave trade)*

3. CHECK UNDERSTANDING

Writing   Ask students to write a brief letter that George Washington might have written to Patrick Henry to convince him to support the Constitution.

Thinking About the Chapter (Making Inferences)   Why do you think the proverb "Half a loaf is better than none" fits the document that the Constitutional Convention created? *(At least it gave the nation a plan that promised to be workable, and it would be open to change through amendment.)*

42 IF YOU CAN KEEP IT

PAGES 186-188

1 Class Period Homework: Student Study Guide p. 48

Chapter Summary

As soon as Americans saw the newly written Constitution, they set out to improve it. The price of ratification was a promise to add the ten amendments known today as the Bill of Rights.

Key Vocabulary

Bill of Rights republic anti-federalist

1. CONNECT

Review with the class the basic conflict that underlay the writing of the Constitution—between setting up a workable central government while trying to protect individual liberties.

2. UNDERSTAND

1. Read pages 186-187 up to "Can you guess what Patrick Henry did...." Discuss: What rights are protected by the Bill of Rights? Ask students to work individually or in teams to paraphrase each amendment. Then invite them to tell why each is important to individual liberty. To reinforce your discussion, you may want to use Resource Page 9 (TG page 117).

2. Read the rest of the chapter. Discuss: Why can we rightly call our nation a republic? *(As citizens, we hold the power to govern, and we exercise that power by electing people who will represent us and carry out what we want government to do.)*

3. Explain to students that the people who opposed ratification of the Constitution were called "anti-federalists," because they were opposed to the federal form of the proposed government. Ask: Why were the anti-federalists opposed to the Constitution? *(Responses should include that they didn't want a powerful central government, wanted the states to be highest power, were concerned about the lack of a Bill of Rights.)*

3. CHECK UNDERSTANDING

Writing Ask students to write a paragraph summarizing the views of the federalists and the anti-federalists, and explaining why the Constitution was finally ratified.

Thinking About the Chapter (Making Predictions) Help the class to recognize that being an American involves both rights and responsibilities. Ask: Will our nation continue to be free and democratic? Will your generation be informed? Will you preserve American democracy? Encourage a focus on the relationship between preserving democracy and being informed citizens.

READING NONFICTION

Analyzing Rhetorical Devices

Remind students that the author has often directed questions to readers and uses the word *you* to address readers. Ask students to write a few sentences telling their personal response to this. Then have students reread the last paragraph of the chapter. Have the class discuss what effect these words had on them. *(Responses should include that all Americans are helping to make American history.)*

MORE ABOUT...

The National Symbol

Refer to the painting *Liberty as Goddess of Youth* on page 188. The bald eagle was initially chosen as the national emblem of the United States in 1782, and became the official symbol in 1787. Its long wingspan and swooping flight made it seem the very essence of freedom. Ben Franklin thought the bald eagle "a bird of bad moral character...and a rank coward." Franklin favored the turkey, which he found "a much more respectable bird...and a bird of courage."

HISTORY ARCHIVES

A History of US Sourcebook

#22, From Alexander Hamilton and James Madison, *The Federalist,* Nos. 1, 10, and 51 (1788)

Ask students to identify ideas in the Federalist Papers that have influenced the system of the U.S. government. *(The Federalist Papers present the authors' ideas about creating a government that was stable and just. They worried about protecting the public from the excesses of rival parties or of an overbearing majority. They desired a strong government with the power to enforce people's rights, but they also recognized the need for devices that controlled the abuses of government. Their concern about the necessity of dividing power among the several departments of government reinforces the system of checks and balances and of separation of power —laid down in the Constitution and upheld to this day.)*

JOHNS HOPKINS TEAM LEARNING

COMPROMISE IN THE CONSTITUTIONAL CONVENTION

1 CLASS PERIOD

FOCUS ACTIVITY

1. Working in teams, have students **Brainstorm** instances in which they themselves are called on to vote. *(Possible responses: for class officers, for club officers, for choosing one activity over another)* How is the voting process a part of the "majority rules" foundation of American society? *(Largest number of votes wins the election.)*

2. In a class discussion, students deal with the fairness of "majority rules." What does it demand of those who do not vote with the majority? *(They must go along with the vote.)* Why might this sometimes be difficult? *(Possible response: The minority might be completely opposed to the majority's decision. Sometimes compromise is difficult to reach.)*

STUDENT TEAM LEARNING ACTIVITY/EVALUATING A COMPROMISE

1. Creating a Situation Tell students that they will stand up to represent the newly emerged American states—some of which are more populous than others—and hold an election on an important matter.

Have ten students stand separately along one side of the classroom, representing the smaller states. Have the rest of the class stand in three groups on the other side of the classroom, representing the large states of Massachusetts, Pennsylvania, and Virginia. Give each small-state student a slip of paper to represent a ballot. Give one ballot to each of the large-state groups. Ask the students to cast their ballots for who will have a week of no homework—the individual students or the groups of students.

2. Discussing the Results When the balloting is complete, ask students how they feel about the election. Was it fair? Why or why not? Tell students that the same problem came up before the Constitutional Convention when delegates had to decide how to give the states fair representation in Congress—how to balance the power of highly populous states with that of smaller states.

Have students read the explanation of this problem in the first three paragraphs on page 172, which explain the Virginia Plan, the New Jersey Plan, and the fairness problem.

3. Finding a Solution Ask students to speculate on how the problem might be solved. Then have them read about the Connecticut Compromise on pages 172-173. Give students an opportunity to discuss whether they think the Connecticut Compromise was fair. Can they think of a better idea?

ASSESSMENT

Part 7 Check-Up   Use Check-Up 7 (TG page 108) to assess learning in Part 7.

ALTERNATE ASSESSMENT
Ask students to write an answer to the following question or complete the suggested activity, which link the big ideas across chapters.

1. Making Connections   Why is an understanding of compromise one of the keys for unlocking the meaning of the Constitution? (Encourage students to explore the role of compromise throughout the debates over the Constitution and the trade-offs that shaped our federal system.)

2. Making Connections   Imagine that you are Andrew Hamilton of Pennsylvania, defender of Peter Zenger. Have a conversation with Alexander Hamilton of New York after the Bill of Rights has been ratified. Discuss the changes that have taken place over time and why they have changed. (*Students should focus on the political climate in which the first Hamilton defended rights of a colonist against English rule versus a time in which independent Americans made their own rules for their future.*)

DEBATING THE ISSUES
Use the topic below to stimulate debate.

Resolved   That the Framers produced the most perfect document that the times would allow. (You might appoint some students to speak for opponents of the document such as George Mason or Patrick Henry. Other students should represent the opinions of Ben Franklin and James Madison. If time allows, have students do additional research into the ratification debate.)

MAKING ETHICAL JUDGMENTS
The following activity asks students to consider issues of ethics.

Imagine you are a delegate to the Constitutional Convention who opposes slavery. Would you, like George Mason, refuse to sign the Constitution? Or would you, like Ben Franklin, place faith in the amendment process and sign it? (To encourage discussion, have students weigh some of the possible outcomes of each decision.)

PROJECTS AND ACTIVITIES
Understanding the Constitution   Provide students with copies (annotated, if possible) of the Constitution. Have them work in small groups to make charts listing the powers given to each of the three branches of government. Post these charts on the wall, and use the data to discuss the system of checks and balances.

USING THE RUBRICS

To assess these writing assignments, group projects, and activities, scoring rubrics have been provided at the back of this Teaching Guide. Be sure to explain the rubrics to your students.

Classifying Information   Have students read and paraphrase all the amendments to the Constitution. Then ask them to categorize the amendments by the kind of change or guarantee that they provide—human rights, rules of government, and so on.

Presenting an Argument   Read aloud the following selection from a letter in which Benjamin Banneker challenges Thomas Jefferson to reexamine his position on slavery.

> *Sir, suffer me to recall to your mind that time in which…the tyranny of the British crown…reduced you to a state of servitude.*

Ask students to complete the letter, presenting arguments in favor of amending the Constitution to abolish slavery.

Illustrating an Idea   Read aloud the quote on page 167 from John Dickinson. Then direct students to draw a poster illustrating Dickinson's ideas on the relationship between the national and state governments. Ask: What aspects of the posters help explain the concept of federalism?

Reenacting History   Request volunteers to find a copy of James Madison's notes on the Constitutional Convention. Using material in this source, students can reenact one of the great debates that helped shape the final document.

Comparing Governments   To help students appreciate the marvel of the system of government set up by the Framers, have them research and report on the systems of government existing in other countries at that time.

Linking Past and Present   Assign a group of students to use the *Readers' Guide to Periodical Literature* to locate articles on the various freedoms protected by the Bill of Rights. Have students arrange precis of these articles on a bulletin board display entitled *The Bill of Rights in Action*.

Who's Who in the News   Divide the class into small groups. Then assign each group to write a social column about the various delegates who have come to Philadelphia. Call on volunteers to read their columns aloud.

Writing Diary Entries   Some delegates brought their families to Philadelphia. Have students imagine that they are one of the delegates' children. Assign them to write diary entries in which they describe their experiences during the summer of 1787.

Designing Historical Posters   Tell students that Independence Hall (the Pennsylvania State House) is now a national monument. Have them imagine that they work for the National Park Service—the agency that oversees the nation's historic sites. Have them make posters explaining the importance of the building to visitors. (If possible, encourage students to do library research for art ideas.)

LOOKING AHEAD

Predicting the Future

Remind students of Benjamin Franklin's admonition to Elizabeth Powel: "A republic, madam. If you can keep it." Then read aloud this statement made by John Marshall, one of the first Chief Justices of the Supreme Court, in 1821:

> *A constitution is framed for ages to come.…Its course cannot always be tranquil. It is exposed to storms and tempest, and its framers must be unwise statesmen indeed if they have not provided it…with the means of self-preservation from the perils it may be destined to encounter.*

Ask students to speculate about what perils they think the new nation will face.

Use the following questions to help students pull together some of the major concepts and themes covered in this book. Note: You may want to assign these as essay questions for assessment.

1. John Adams said, "The Revolution was affected before the war commenced." Do you agree with him or do you think there was some way to avoid the conflict? *(Students who agree with Adams should cite attitudes, opinions, or events that show a movement toward revolution long before the first bullets were fired. Students who disagree should point to instances in which compromise might have avoided war. They might mention the large number of people who did not form an opinion until the bullets at Lexington and Concord forced them to do so.)*

2. When Thomas Jefferson went off to write the Declaration of Independence, he said it was not the time "to invent new ideas." Instead, he promised to make the document "an expression of the American mind." Based on your knowledge of the Declaration of Independence, what long-standing ideas or opinions might have influenced Jefferson? *(Students should hark back to the rights of Englishmen, Enlightenment ideas about the natural rights of humankind, and Americans' growing spirit of independence.)*

3. What was the immediate cause of the American Revolution? What were the deeper, underlying causes? *(Most students will name the battles of Lexington and Concord as the immediate cause. Underlying causes might include conflicts over taxes, British efforts to control westward expansion, abuses of royal power, and so on. The important point is that conflicts built up over time.)*

4. Hector St. John Crevecoeur called America the "most perfect society in the world." How did the Constitution help support this claim? How did the Constitution prove Crevecoeur wrong? *(Provisions for self-government and guarantees of individual liberty help support Crevecoeur. However, the inclusion of slavery in the Constitution and its failure to deal fairly—or at all—with Native Americans, and the lack of rights for women show limits to his description.)*

5. What changes did the American Revolution bring to the world? *(Possible responses: It ushered in the world's first federal republic; its success encouraged people elsewhere in the world to try to win liberty for themselves; it created a nation that would one day become a superpower in the world.)*

6. Despite all the changes ushered in by the Revolution, the war also ensured the continuity of certain American ideals. What are some of these, and how do they affect your life today? *(Students should name government by consent of the governed, equality before the law, the guarantees of the Bill of Rights—like freedom of religion, speech, press, and assembly. They should also offer examples of these ideals in action today—the election of representatives, actions against discrimination, the many churches in any community, the variety of news media protected from government oppression, and so on.)*

SYNTHESIZING THE BIG IDEAS IN BOOK THREE

GROUP ASSESSMENT

In addition to, or instead of, some or all of these essay questions, consider a culminating activity in which groups of students closely study the three documents pivotal to our government's foundation. Divide the class into small groups and direct them to use a three-column chart. In the left column, they should list the principles in the Declaration of Independence. In the center column, the applicable principles in the Articles of Confederation. In the right column, the applicable principles in the Constitution. Students should use information from Book 3 and the Sourcebook for research. Encourage the groups to discuss and debate as they delve into the words of these documents. Use the rubrics at the back of this guide for assessment. (Note: This activity will involve several class periods.)

CHECK-UP 1

Answering the following questions will help you understand and remember what you have read in Chapters 1-6. Write your answers on a separate sheet of paper.

1. The pairs of people listed below played key roles in events described in Chapters 1-6. Tell who each person was and what he did of importance in this period. Describe the connections between the two people in each pair.
    a. Peter Zenger, Andrew Hamilton
    b. George Washington, Edward Braddock
    c. William Johnson, Jeffrey Amherst

2. What happened at each of these places? What effects did the events have on actions that followed?
    a. Fort Duquesne
    b. Albany
    c. Quebec

3. Define each of the following terms. Then explain its significance to the events of the time.
    a. libel
    b. Iroquois League
    c. Albany conference
    d. missions

4. What did Benjamin Franklin think that the colonists could learn from the Iroquois?

5. Representatives from the British colonies and the Iroquois League met in Albany and later at the home of William Johnson. Imagine that you are a reporter who has been at both meetings. Write a short news analysis comparing the two conferences. Comment on which meeting you think was more successful, and why.

6. Write a summary of the French and Indian War, including the events at Fort Duquesne, the Albany conference, Lake George, Louisbourg, and Quebec.

7. Explain the effects of the Treaty of Paris and the end of the war on each of the following groups living in North America.
    a. French people
    b. Spanish people
    c. Native Americans

8. Describe one person you have read about whom you admire. Tell what actions or opinions of that person you particularly respect, and why.

9. Choose one event from this time at which you would have liked to be present. Tell why you would like to have been there and what you would have done.

10. **Thinking About the Big Ideas** What conflicts did the British colonists face in this period? What changes occurred as a result of these conflicts?

CHECK-UP 2

Answering the following questions will help you understand and remember what you have read in Chapters 7-10. Write your answers on a separate sheet of paper.

1. The people listed below played key roles in events described in Chapters 7-10. Tell who each person was and what he or she did of importance in this period.
   a. Sir William Johnson
   b. Daniel Boone
   c. Hector St. John Crevecoeur
   d. Eliza Lucas Pinckney

2. How did geography affect the growth of the colonies? Tell what role each of the following geographical features played in the movement of people in the colonies and how each contributed to colonists' feelings of independence.
   a. Appalachian Mountains
   b. Ohio River valley
   c. Cumberland Gap

3. Define each of the following terms. Then explain its significance to the events of the time.
   a. Great Awakening
   b. Proclamation of 1763
   c. pioneer
   d. yeoman farmer
   e. indigo
   f. habeus corpus

4. Hector St. John Crevecoeur believed that Americans were a new kind of people. Explain how Crevecoeur thought colonial Americans differed from people in the Old World.

5. Imagine that you are a reporter from England, visiting Eliza Lucas Pinckney. You have heard about her indigo crop and want to find out more about this independent-minded American. Make notes for your article.

6. British citizens—whether in Britain or in America—took certain rights for granted. What part did the following play in gaining those rights?
   a. Magna Carta
   b. Glorious Revolution

7. Imagine that you live on the frontier west of the Appalachian Mountains. Write a letter to someone on the East Coast. Tell the person how you feel about your ability to take care of yourself and make your own rules.

8. **Thinking About the Big Ideas**   What changes led to a more independent spirit among the colonists? How could this lead to conflict with England?

CHECK-UP 3

Answering the following questions will help you understand and remember what you have read in Chapters 11-15. Write your answers on a separate sheet of paper.

1. The people listed below played key roles in events described in Chapters 11-15. Tell how the people in each group are connected and what each one did that was important in this period.
   a. King George III, Charles Townshend, Lord North
   b. Samuel Adams, Thomas Paine, Patrick Henry
   c. Captain Thomas Preston, Paul Revere, Crispus Attucks, John Adams
   d. Paul Revere, William Dawes, Samuel Prescott, Captain John Parker
   e. Ethan Allen, Benedict Arnold
   f. Isaac Newton, John Locke, Jean-Jacques Rousseau

2. In the years before the American Revolution, a number of important events took place in and around Boston. Tell where each event below took place and why it happened in that location.
   a. Boston Tea Party
   b. Boston Massacre
   c. Battles of Lexington and Concord

3. Define each of the following terms. Then explain its significance to the events of the time.
   a. Haudenosaunee
   b. Committees of Correspondence
   c. Continental army
   d. Quartering Act
   e. Continental Congress

4. The colonists said "No taxation without representation." What did they mean by that? How did England tax the colonies and how did the colonies react?

5. How did geography affect transportation and communication in the colonies?

6. Compare the points of view of a British soldier, a colonist, and John Adams on the Boston Massacre.

7. Describe the sequence of events from the time New Englanders stockpiled munitions at Concord to the battle in Lexington on April 19, 1775. Imagine that you were there, and write your description as diary entries.

8. **Thinking About the Big Ideas** Between the end of the French and Indian War and the battles of Lexington and Concord, what changed about the colonists and their relationship with England? How did a conflict of ideas become a conflict of weapons?

CHECK-UP 4

Answering the following questions will help you understand and remember what you have read in Chapters 16-21. Write your answers on a separate sheet of paper.

1. Of all of the delegates present at the Second Continental Congress, some were outstanding. Tell what each of the men below did of importance at the congress.
   a. George Washington
   b. Thomas Jefferson
   c. John Hancock
   d. John Adams
   e. Benjamin Franklin

2. Choose three other delegates to the Second Continental Congress. Tell something about their beliefs and qualifications as delegates.

3. The geography of the Boston area was a factor in the Battle of Bunker Hill. Identify the following places and describe the role each played in the battle.
   a. Charles River
   b. Charlestown
   c. Breed's Hill

4. Geography also played a role at the Battle of Charleston. What was the importance of each of the following in that battle?
   a. Charleston Harbor
   b. Sullivan's Island
   c. shoals
   d. palmetto trees

5. Define each of the following terms. Then explain its significance to the events of the time.
   a. militia
   b. congress
   c. Olive Branch Petition
   d. a "John Hancock"
   e. consent of the governed

6. War had not yet been declared when the Second Continental Congress met in May 1776. What preparations were made for fighting and why did the delegates believe they were necessary?

7. Explain how the battles of Bunker Hill and Charleston gave the colonists confidence.

8. **Thinking About the Big Ideas**   In a declaration, the writers state something in a stirring manner. In the Declaration of Independence, what did the delegates state about the following points?
   a. independence
   b. King George III
   c. equality
   d. rights
   e. consent of the governed

CHECK-UP 5

Answering the following questions will help you understand and remember what you have read in Chapters 22-28. Write your answers on a separate sheet of paper.

1. Imagine a conversation between the two people in each pair below. Identify each person and tell what he or she did during the American Revolution. Write a few sentences that they might have said to each other.
   a. Molly Pitcher, Molly Brant
   b. Martha Washington, Abigail Adams
   c. Marquis de Lafayette, Baron von Steuben
   d. General John Burgoyne, General Horatio Gates
   e. George Washington, George Rogers Clark

2. If you were drawing a map about the American Revolution, why would you show the places below on your map? How was each important in the war?
   a. New York, New York
   b. Trenton, New Jersey
   c. Saratoga, New York
   d. Valley Forge, Pennsylvania
   e. the Ohio River valley

3. Why does the author use the term *people's war* to describe the American Revolution? Here are three clues—use them in your explanation: women, children, and slaves fought; citizen soldiers; the spirit of Valley Forge.

4. Imagine that you could interview James Forten. What would he say about the following?
   a. why he supported the colonists
   b. what he did during the war
   c. how and why he remained an American

5. Compare the help of the Marquis de Lafayette and Haym Salomon.

6. You are a British soldier with General Burgoyne. Describe your adventures from Lake Champlain until you sail away from Boston.

7. In what ways was George Washington a great leader on and off the battlefield?

8. **Thinking About the Big Ideas** The Battle of Saratoga is often called the turning point in the American Revolution. What changed as a result of that battle? Compare Americans' feelings after this battle with their feelings after the Battle of Bunker Hill.

CHECK-UP 6

Answering the following questions will help you understand and remember what you have read in Chapters 29-34. Write your answers on a separate sheet of paper.

1. The people listed below played key roles in the Battle of Yorktown. Tell who each person was and what he did in the battle. For groups of names, explain their connection to one another.
    a. Lord Charles Cornwallis, General Henry Clinton
    b. Admiral de Grasse
    c. Comte de Rochambeau, George Washington
    d. Marquis de Lafayette, Baron von Steuben, General Anthony Wayne
    e. Alexander Hamilton

2. Important changes were happening west of the Appalachians. Describe the changes that occurred in each set of present-day states.
    a. California, New Mexico, Arizona, Texas
    b. Ohio, Illinois, Indiana, Michigan, Wisconsin, Minnesota

3. Two "separations" were an essential part of the plan for the new nation. Explain the meaning and significance of the following terms.
    a. separation of powers
    b. separation of church and state

4. In what ways does the story of Mary Katherine Goddard reflect major issues of the time? Discuss in terms of the following:
    a. independence
    b. freedom of the press
    c. women's rights
    d. slavery

5. The Articles of Confederation gave most power to the states and little power to the national government. What problems did this cause in the following areas?
    a. voting in Congress
    b. levying taxes
    c. military forces
    d. national loyalty

6. The Northwest Ordinance set up a pattern of statehood that would be followed as the nation grew. Answer the following questions about the ordinance.
    a. Who passed the ordinance?
    b. Why was it passed?
    c. Where was the Northwest Territory and who had claimed the land before?
    d. What states were eventually created from the territory?
    e. What was guaranteed to settlers?

7. Conduct an imaginary interview with Thomas Jefferson. Decide what questions you would most like to have asked him and write the responses you think he might have given.

8. **Thinking About the Big Ideas**   Why did the unity Americans felt during the Revolution change to a new kind of conflict after the war?

CHECK-UP 7

Answering the following questions will help you understand and remember what you have read in Chapters 35-42. Write your answers on a separate sheet of paper.

1. Of all of the delegates to the Constitutional Convention, James Madison may have been the most important. In fact, he has been called the Father of the Constitution. His views and his role at the convention are described throughout these chapters. Review what is written about Madison. Then write a summary called "James Madison at the Constitutional Convention."

2. Choose three other delegates to the Constitutional Convention. Tell something about their qualifications as Framers. Describe their beliefs about the best government for the new nation.

3. Define each of these terms. Then explain its significance in the creation of a new plan of government.
   a. confederation
   b. federation
   c. legislature
   d. executive
   e. judiciary
   f. houses
   g. amendment
   h. ratify

4. The following phrases stand for ideas that are central to the American form of government. Imagine that you are explaining our government to someone from another country. Use these three ideas in your explanation.
   a. unalienable rights
   b. consent of the governed
   c. checks and balances

5. Explain the details of the Virginia Plan and the New Jersey Plan, and how the Connecticut Compromise saved the Constitution.

6. The question of slavery raised powerful emotions at the convention. Describe the arguments each of the following Framers would have made.
   a. One who wanted to outlaw slavery
   b. One who wanted to keep slavery
   c. One who believed a compromise was necessary

7. George Mason was one of the Framers who refused to sign the final document. Patrick Henry fought hard against ratification. Describe their reasons. Then compare them to the arguments for the Constitution made by James Madison and Benjamin Franklin.

8. **Thinking About the Big Ideas** What conflicts had to be resolved in order to change the government from a confederation of equal states to a federal system?

RESOURCE PAGE 1

Changing Territorial Claims

Directions: Use information you have learned about how Britain, France, and Spain battled for territory in North America to fill in the outline map below.

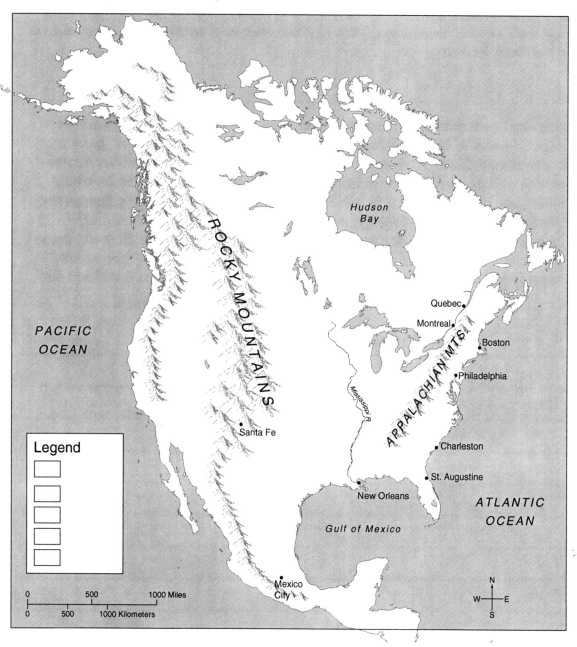

1. Using three differently colored pencils, fill in the areas claimed by each nation about 1750. Draw a map legend showing the color for each nation.

2. By 1763, France had lost its territory in North America. Draw hatch marks (diagonal lines) showing this territory. For land that went to Spain, draw the lines from upper left to lower right. For England, draw them from upper right to lower left.

RESOURCE PAGE 2

The Adventures of Daniel Boone

Directions: Read how the pathfinder Daniel Boone described the wilderness west of the Appalachian Mountains. (His words might sound a bit high-flown for a hardy frontiersman. A writer named Gilbert Imlay polished up Boone's language, but he kept Boone's wonder at what he saw.) Then, on the lines below, write a paragraph in which you give specific reasons why American settlers would be anxious to start new lives in the West.

> *One day I undertook a tour through the country, and the [variety] and beauties of nature I met with in this charming season, expelled every gloomy and [troublesome] thought....Not a breeze shook [a] leaf. I had gained the summit of a commanding ridge, and, looking round with astonishing delight, beheld the ample plains, the beauteous tracts below. On the other hand, I surveyed the famous river Ohio, that rolled in silent dignity, marking the western boundary of Kentucky with inconceivable grandeur. At a vast distance I beheld the mountains lift their...brows and penetrate the clouds. All things were still. I kindled a fire near a fountain of sweet water, and feasted on a loin of a buck, which a few hours before I had killed.*

_____

_____

_____

_____

_____

_____

_____

_____

_____

_____

_____

_____

_____

Name _____   **Date** _____

RESOURCE PAGE 3

Following the King's Highway

Directions: The major route between Boston and New York City in colonial times was the Boston Post Road. In time, it became part of a road network called the King's Highway. Study the map below and then answer the questions about it.

1. About how many miles long was the King's Highway? _____

2. Through which colonies did the King's Highway pass?

   _____

   _____

3. Travel by wagon along the King's Highway averaged 20-25 miles per day. If your wagon travels 20 miles a day, how long would it take you to go from New York City to Philadelphia?

   _____

4. If your wagon travels 25 miles a day, how long would it take you to travel the entire distance from Boston to Charleston?

   _____

RESOURCE PAGE 4

Population of the English Colonies

Directions: Study the chart of estimated populations of the English colonies in 1770, and then complete the activities that follow.

New Hampshire 62,000	New Jersey 117,000	Virginia 447,000
Massachusetts 267,000	Pennsylvania 240,000	North Carolina 197,000
Rhode Island 58,000	Delaware 36,000	South Carolina 124,000
Connecticut 184,000	Maryland 203,000	Georgia 24,000
New York 163,000		

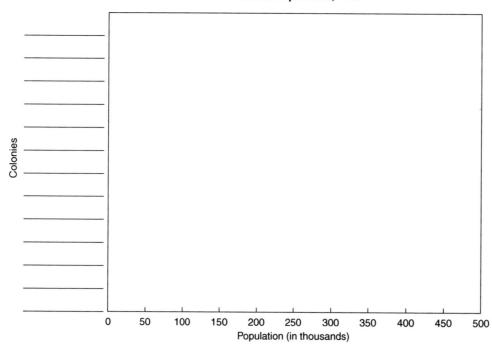

Colonial Population, 1770

Colonies

0   50   100   150   200   250   300   350   400   450   500
Population (in thousands)

A. Use the information in the chart to make a horizontal bar graph of the colonial populations. Order the colonies from largest at the top to smallest at the bottom.

B. On the lines below, write two riddles using the populations of different colonies. Exchange papers with a partner and answer each other's riddles.

1. _____

_____

2. _____

_____

RESOURCE PAGE 5

The Battle of Bunker Hill

Directions: Reread the account in your textbook of "The War of the Hills" (Chapter 18), especially the illustration on pages 90-91. Using the information in the text and the map below, complete the activity.

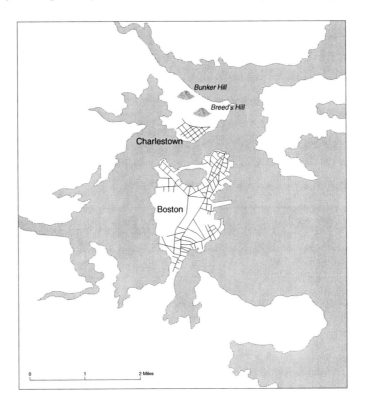

1. On the map, draw a blue line showing the Patriots' fortifications on Breed's Hill. Then draw a red arrow showing the route the British took to attack Breed's Hill.

2. According to the illustration on pages 90-91, what else besides soldiers did the British use to attack the Patriot lines?

_____

_____

_____

3. The author says that the British probably should have attacked the Patriots from a different direction. On the map, draw a dotted red line showing a possible route. Then write a sentence or two speculating why the British decided to attack head on.

_____

_____

_____

RESOURCE PAGE 6

Costs of the American Revolution

Directions: What were the costs of the Revolution to Americans—in people who served in it, in casualties and deaths, and in dollars? Work with the figures below to calculate these costs.

Population of American colonies: 2,750,000 (approximate)
Number of Americans who enrolled in military service: 200,000
Americans killed in combat: 4,435
Americans wounded in combat: 6,188
Cost of war for Americans (in today's dollars): $1,200,000,000

1. What percentage of the entire population enrolled in military service during the Revolution? _____

2. What is the total number of Americans killed or wounded during the Revolution? _____

3. What percent of all those enrolled in military service were killed or wounded? _____

4. Imagine that the costs of the war were spread evenly across the entire population of the 13 states. What would be the cost for each man, woman, and child in the United States?

_____

5. Using the figures above, write an explanation of why Congress's inability to raise money through taxes was almost disastrous to the American war effort.

_____

_____

_____

_____

RESOURCE PAGE 7

The Battle of Yorktown

Directions: The map at right shows events surrounding the decisive Battle of Yorktown (textbook pages 143-146). Use information from the map and from your textbook to answer the questions below.

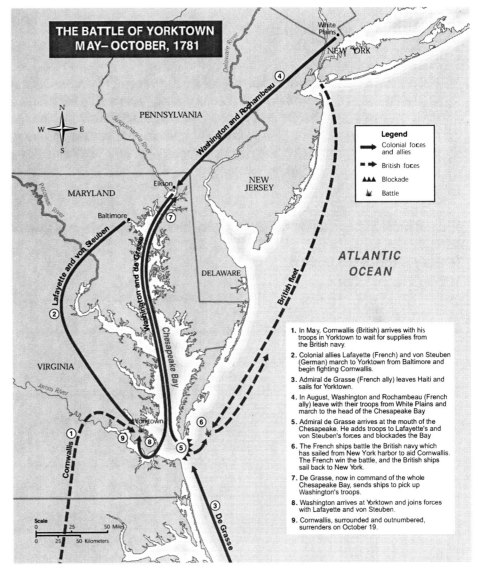

THE BATTLE OF YORKTOWN MAY– OCTOBER, 1781

Legend
- Colonial forces and allies
- British forces
- Blockade
- Battle

1. In May, Cornwallis (British) arrives with his troops in Yorktown to wait for supplies from the British navy.
2. Colonial allies Lafayette (French) and von Steuben (German) march to Yorktown from Baltimore and begin fighting Cornwallis.
3. Admiral de Grasse (French ally) leaves Haiti and sails for Yorktown.
4. In August, Washington and Rochambeau (French ally) leave with their troops from White Plains and march to the head of the Chesapeake Bay
5. Admiral de Grasse arrives at the mouth of the Chesapeake. He adds troops to Lafayette's and von Steuben's forces and blockades the Bay
6. The French ships battle the British navy which has sailed from New York harbor to aid Cornwallis. The French win the battle, and the British ships sail back to New York.
7. De Grasse, now in command of the whole Chesapeake Bay, sends ships to pick up Washington's troops.
8. Washington arrives at Yorktown and joins forces with Lafayette and von Steuben.
9. Cornwallis, surrounded and outnumbered, surrenders on October 19.

1. On the map, what two rivers is Yorktown between? What other large body of water is nearby?

_____

2. Why did Cornwallis choose this location near water for his base?

_____

3. Using the map scale, estimate how far Washington's troops had to march to get to Yorktown. It took them about 40 days. Approximately how many miles did they travel per day?

_____

4. Why did Yorktown turn into a trap for Cornwallis?

_____

RESOURCE PAGE 8

The Constitution's Answer to the Declaration of Independence

Directions: The Declaration of Independence cited grievances that the colonists had against King George III. The Constitution was written to ensure that these grievances did not occur in the United States. Four of these grievances are given below. Each is followed by a reference to the Constitutional provision addressing it. Read each grievance. Then go to the Constitution on pages 194-199 in your textbook. Locate the reference in the Constitution following each grievance. Then write an explanation of how it corrects the grievance.

1. **Declaration of Independence:** He has forbidden his Government to pass Laws of immediate and pressing Importance....
   Constitution: Article I, Section 1

   _____

   _____

   _____

2. **Declaration of Independence:** He has refused for a long Time [after dissolving Representative Houses] to cause others to be elected....
   Constitution: Article I, Section 4

   _____

   _____

   _____

3. **Declaration of Independence:** He has obstructed the Administration of Justice, by refusing his Assent of Laws for establishing Judiciary Powers.
   Constitution: Article 3, Section 1

   _____

   _____

   _____

4. **Declaration of Independence:** He has affected to render the Military independent of and superior to the Civil Power.
   Constitution: Article II, first paragraph

   _____

   _____

   _____

RESOURCE PAGE 9

Constitution and Bill of Rights Checkup

Directions: Part I leads you on a search through the Constitution (textbook pages 194-199). Part II asks you to compare abuses of rights named in the Declaration of Independence with guarantees in the Bill of Rights.

Part I

Answer the questions about the system of government created by the Constitution. In the blanks, write the number of the Article and Section of the Constitution where the answer can be found. (Some Articles do not have Sections.)

1. How many representatives are there?

   Article _____ Section _____

2. What is the Senate?

   Article _____ Section _____

3. Which branch has the power to tax?

   Article _____ Section _____

4. Who can be President?

   Article _____ Section _____

5. What military and civil powers does the President have?

   Article _____ Section _____

6. What cases does the Supreme Court hear?

   Article _____ Section _____

7. How shall new states enter the Union?

   Article _____ Section _____

8. What amendments are forbidden?

   Article _____ Section _____

9. What law is supreme in the nation?

   Article _____ Section _____

10. How was the Constitution to be ratified?

    Article _____ Section _____

Part II

In the Declaration of Independence, colonists listed their complaints against King George III. Compare each of the complaints below with the rights guaranteed in the Bill of Rights (textbook page 199). In each blank, list the Amendment that protects Americans against this abuse. (Not all the Amendments will be used.)

1. He has refused his assent to laws for the public good.

   Amendment _____

2. He has dissolved representative houses repeatedly.

   Amendment _____

3. He had made judges dependent on his will alone.

   Amendment _____

4. He has sent swarms of officers to harass our people and eat their [food].

   Amendment _____

5. He has transported us beyond the sea to be tried for pretended offenses.

   Amendment _____

On a separate sheet of paper, write a short paragraph beginning with this topic sentence: *Americans made every effort to protect themselves against abuses of power by the government.*

USING THE
MAP RESOURCE PAGES

These maps are provided for use with class projects and activities:

Reproducible Colonial Era Map*
Project suggestion: Use the map with the ongoing "Using Maps: Colonial Era Map" project suggested on TG page 30. Have students create a geographical overview of important events and locations from the colonial era as they read the book.

Reproducible Revolutionary Relief Map*
Project suggestion: Use this with the "Using Maps: Revolutionary War Room Map" activity described on TG pages 30–31. Have students trace battles, routes, events and outcomes from the Revolutionary War as they read the book.

Reproducible Eastern US Relief Map*
Project suggestion: Use this map as an alternate to the maps above.

Also, use this map with the "Geography Connections" activities in Chapters 32–33. Have students sketch the land claims made by the new States, and the effects of the Northwest Ordinance. Alternately, use the Blank US Political Map w/ State Borders or US Relief Map.

Reproducible US Political Comparison Map*
Project suggestion: Use this map with the two-part activity that begins with Chapter 2 "Geography Connections" and ends with the Part 6 opener "Linking Geography and Politics." Have students sketch and compare changes in European control of North America, comparing the colonial period to the Treaty of Paris agreements.

Reproducible Blank US Political Map w/ State Borders*
Project suggestion: Use this map as an alternate to the Eastern US Relief Map or US Relief Map in activites described above.

* These maps are also printed in each Student Study Guide for *From Colonies to Country.*

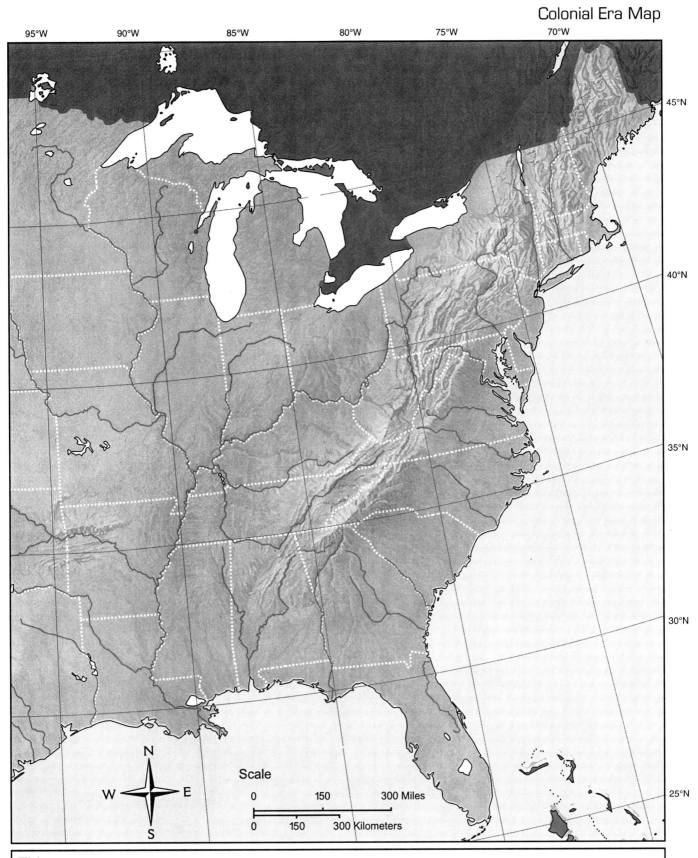

95°W   90°W   85°W   80°W   75°W   70°W

45°N

40°N

35°N

30°N

25°N

Scale

N
W — E
S

0   150   300 Miles

0   150   300 Kilometers

Title

Legend

Revolutionary War Relief Map

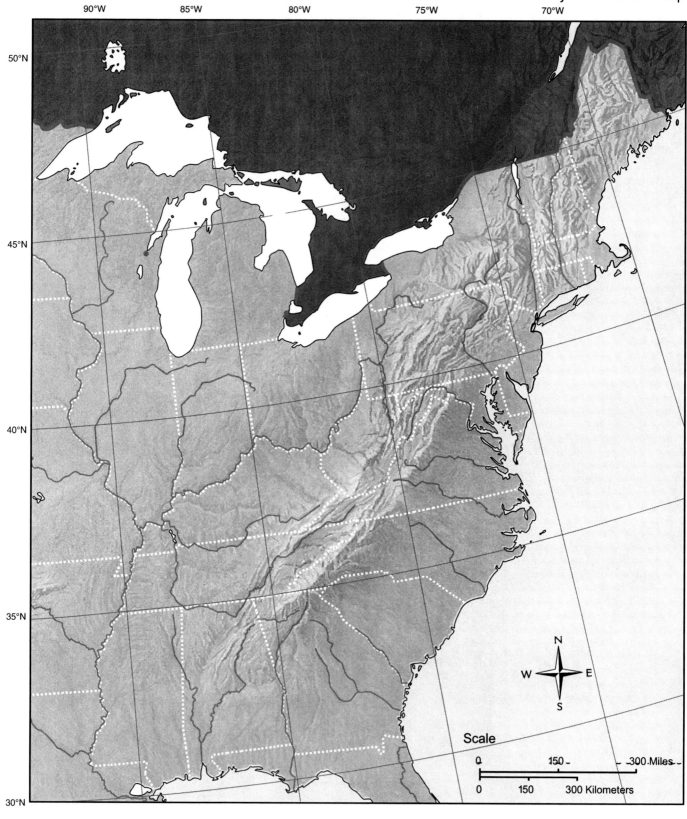

90°W   85°W   80°W   75°W   70°W

50°N

45°N

40°N

35°N

30°N

N
W   E
S

Scale

0   150   300 Miles

0   150   300 Kilometers

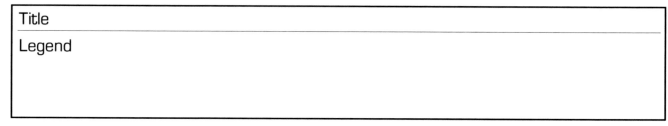

Title

Legend

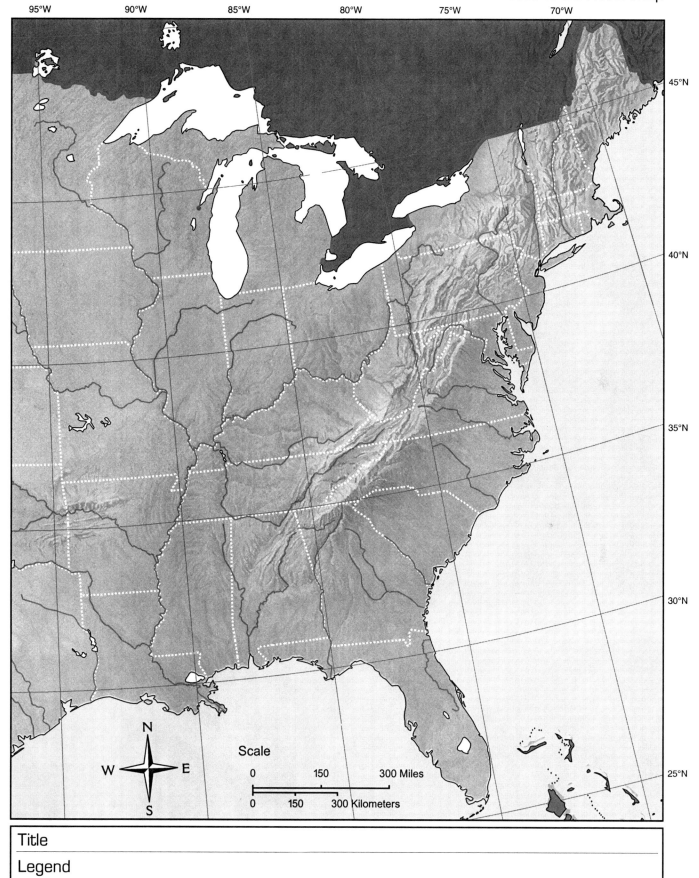

Eastern US Relief Map

95°W   90°W   85°W   80°W   75°W   70°W

45°N

40°N

35°N

30°N

25°N

N
W   E
S

Scale
0   150   300 Miles

0   150   300 Kilometers

Title

Legend

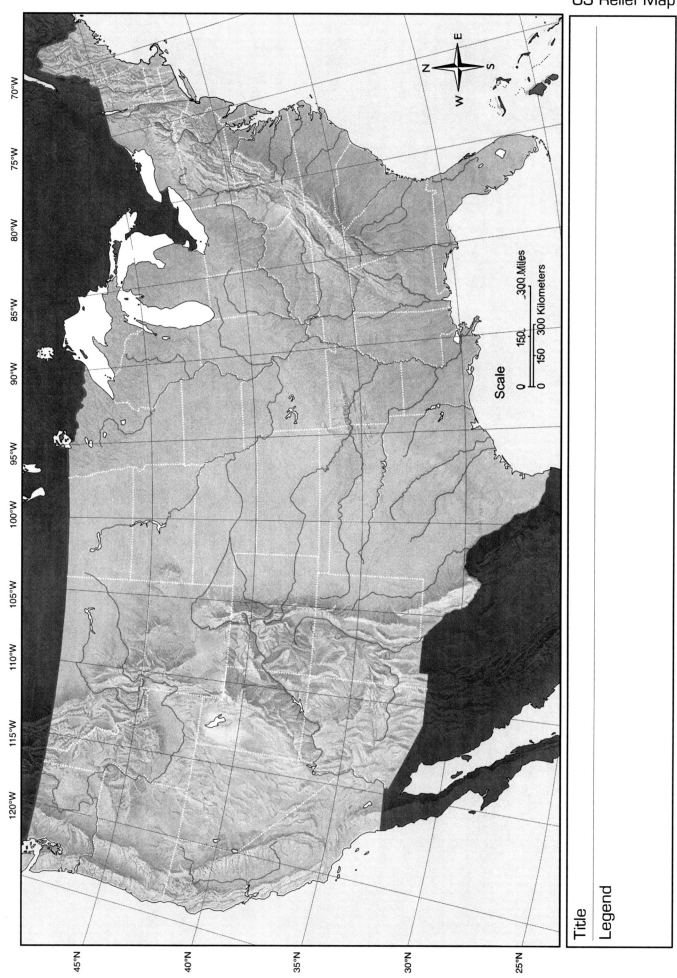

Scale

300 Miles
150
0

300 Kilometers
150
0

Title

Legend

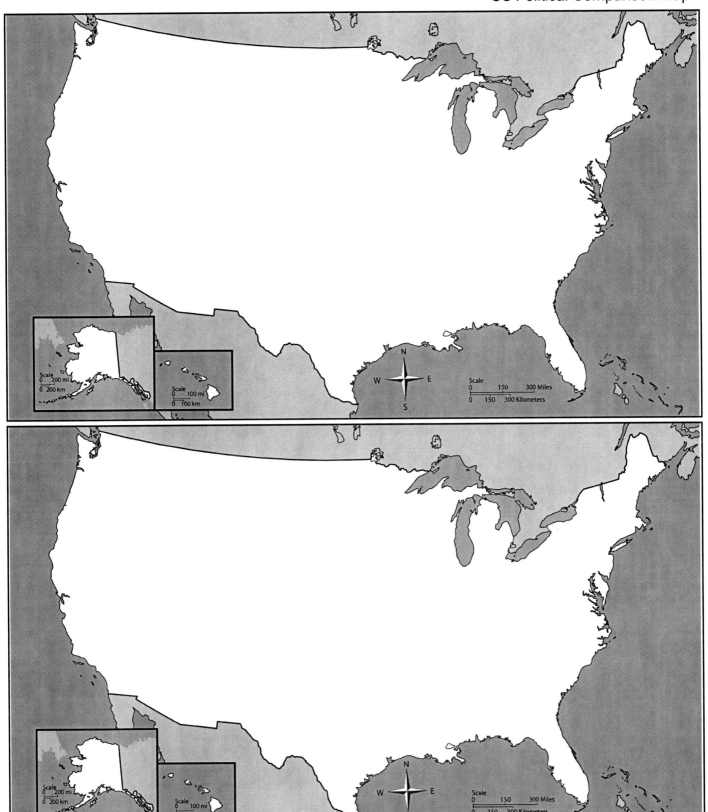

Scale
0   200 mi
0   200 km

Scale
0   100 mi
0   100 km

N
W   E
S

Scale
0   150   300 Miles
0   150   300 Kilometers

Scale
0   200 mi
0   200 km

Scale
0   100 mi
0   100 km

N
W   E
S

Scale
0   150   300 Miles
0   150   300 Kilometers

Title

Legend

Blank US Political Map w/ State Borders

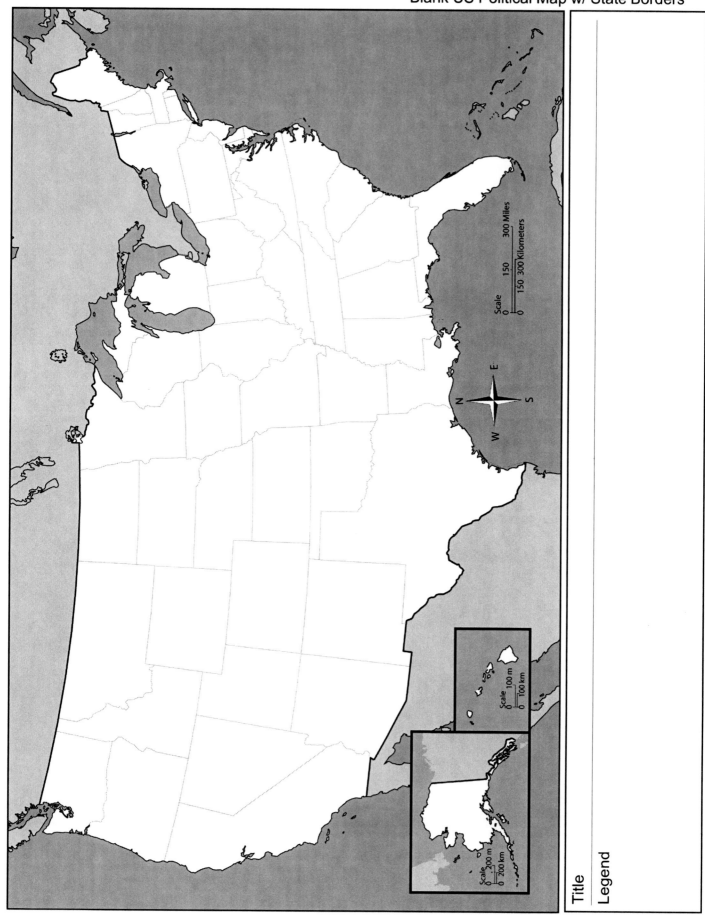

Scale
0   150   300 Miles
0   150   300 Kilometers

Scale
0   100 m
0   100 km

Scale
0   200 m
0   200 km

N E S W

Title

Legend

SCORING RUBRIC

The reproducibles on the following pages have been adapted from this rubric for use as handouts and a student self-scoring activity, with added focus on planning, cooperation, revision and presentation. You may wish to tailor the self-scoring activity—for example, asking students to comment on how low scores could be improved, or focusing only on specific rubric points. Use the Library/Media Center Research Log to help students focus and evaluate their research for projects and assignments.

As with any rubric, you should introduce and explain the rubric before students begin their assignments. The more thoroughly your students understand how they will be evaluated, the better prepared they will be to produce projects that fulfill your expectations.

	ORGANIZATION	CONTENT	ORAL/WRITTEN CONVENTIONS	GROUP PARTICIPATION
4	• Clearly addresses all parts of the writing task. • Demonstrates a clear understanding of purpose and audience. • Maintains a consistent point of view, focus, and organizational structure, including the effective use of transitions. • Includes a clearly presented central idea with relevant facts, details, and/or explanations.	• Demonstrates that the topic was well researched. • Uses only information that was essential and relevant to the topic. • Presents the topic thoroughly and accurately. • Reaches reasonable conclusions clearly based on evidence.	• Contains few, if any, errors in grammar, punctuation, capitalization, or spelling. • Uses a variety of sentence types. • Speaks clearly, using effective volume and intonation.	• Demonstrated high levels of participation and effective decision making. • Planned well and used time efficiently. • Demonstrated ability to negotiate opinions fairly and reach compromise when needed. • Utilized effective visual aids.
3	• Addresses all parts of the writing task. • Demonstrates a general understanding of purpose and audience. • Maintains a mostly consistent point of view, focus, and organizational structure, including the effective use of some transitions. • Presents a central idea with mostly relevant facts, details, and/or explanations.	• Demonstrates that the topic was sufficiently researched. • Uses mainly information that was essential and relevant to the topic. • Presents the topic accurately but leaves some aspects unexplored. • Reaches reasonable conclusions loosely related to evidence.	• Contains some errors in grammar, punctuation, capitalization, or spelling. • Uses a variety of sentence types. • Speaks somewhat clearly, using effective volume and intonation.	• Demonstrated good participation and decision making with few distractions. • Planning and used its time acceptably. • Demonstrated ability to negotiate opinions and compromise with little aggression or unfairness.
2	• Addresses only parts of the writing task. • Demonstrates little understanding of purpose and audience. • Maintains an inconsistent point of view, focus, and/or organizational structure, which may include ineffective or awkward transitions that do not unify important ideas. • Suggests a central idea with limited facts, details, and/or explanations.	• Demonstrates that the topic was minimally researched. • Uses a mix of relevant and irrelevant information. • Presents the topic with some factual errors and leaves some aspects unexplored. • Reaches conclusions that do not stem from evidence presented in the project.	• Contains several errors in grammar, punctuation, capitalization, or spelling. These errors may interfere with the reader's understanding of the writing. • Uses little variety in sentence types. • Speaks unclearly or too quickly. May interfere with the audience's understanding of the project.	• Demonstrated uneven participation or was often off-topic. Task distribution was lopsided. • Did not show a clear plan for the project, and did not use time well. • Allowed one or two opinions to dominate the activity, or had trouble reaching a fair consensus.
1	• Addresses only one part of the writing task. • Demonstrates no understanding of purpose and audience. • Lacks a point of view, focus, organizational structure, and transitions that unify important ideas. • Lacks a central idea but may contain marginally related facts, details, and/or explanations.	• Demonstrates that the topic was poorly researched. • Does not discriminate relevant from irrelevant information. • Presents the topic incompletely, with many factual errors. • Did not reach conclusions.	• Contains serious errors in grammar, punctuation, capitalization, or spelling. These errors interfere with the reader's understanding of the writing. • Uses no sentence variety. • Speaks unclearly. The audience must struggle to understand the project.	• Demonstrated poor participation by the majority of the group. Tasks were completed by a small minority. • Failed to show planning or effective use of time. • Was dominated by a single voice, or allowed hostility to derail the project.

NAME _____   **PROJECT** _____

DATE _____

ORGANIZATION & FOCUS	CONTENT	ORAL/WRITTEN-CONVENTIONS	GROUP PARTICI-PATION

COMMENTS AND SUGGESTIONS

UNDERSTANDING YOUR SCORE

Organization: Your project should be clear, focused on a main idea, and organized. You should use details and facts to support your main idea.

Content: You should use strong research skills. Your project should be thorough and accurate.

Oral/Written Conventions: For writing projects, you should use good composition, grammar, punctuation, and spelling, with a good variety of sentence types. For oral projects, you should engage the class using good public speaking skills.

Group Participation: Your group should cooperate fairly and use its time well to plan, assign and revise the tasks involved in the project.

NAME _____ **GROUP MEMBERS** _____

_____

_____

_____

Use this worksheet to describe your project by finishing the sentences below.
For individual projects and writing assignments, use the "How I did" section.
For group projects, use both "How I did" and "How we did" sections.

The purpose of this project is to :

[ ]

Scoring Key = **4** – extremely well
3 – well
2 – could have been better
1 – not well at all

HOW I DID

I understood the purpose and requirements for this project...

I planned and organized my time and work...

This project showed clear organization that emphasized the central idea...

I supported my point with details and description...

I polished and revised this project...

I utilized correct grammar and good writing/speaking style...

Overall, this project met its purpose...

HOW WE DID

We divided up tasks...

We cooperated and listened to each other...

We talked through what we didn't understand...

We used all our time to make this project the best it could be...

Overall, as a group we worked together...

I contributed and cooperated with the team...

LIBRARY/ MEDIA CENTER RESEARCH LOG

NAME _____

DUE DATE _____

What I Need to **Find**

I need to use: ☐ primary / ☐ secondary sources.

Places I **Know** to Look

Brainstorm: Other Sources and Places to Look

WHAT I FOUND

Title/Author/Location (call # or URL)

How I Found it

Suggestion / Library Catalog / Browsing / Internet Search / Web link

Primary Source / Secondary Source

Book/Periodical / Website / Other

Rate each source from 1 (low) to 4 (high) in the categories below

helpful   relevant

OUTLINE

MAIN IDEA: _____

_____

_____

    DETAIL: _____

_____

    DETAIL: _____

_____

    DETAIL: _____

_____

MAIN IDEA: _____

_____

_____

    DETAIL: _____

_____

    DETAIL: _____

_____

    DETAIL: _____

_____

Name _____ Date _____

MAIN IDEA MAP

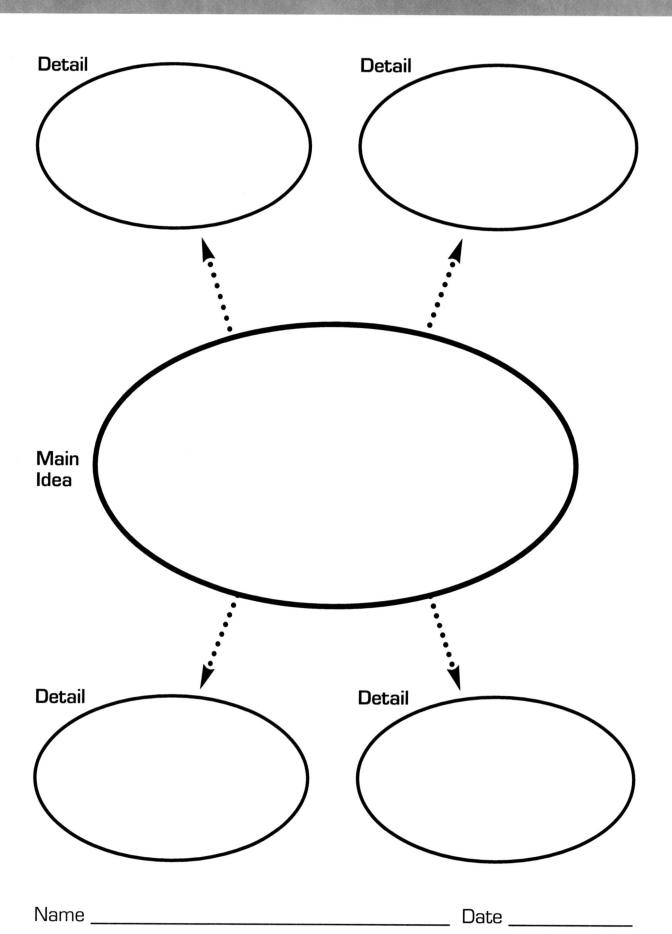

Detail

Detail

Main Idea

Detail

Detail

Name _____ Date _____

K-W-L CHART

K	W	L
What I Know	What I Want to Know	What I Learned

Name _____ Date _____

VENN DIAGRAM

Write differences in the circles. Write similarities where the circles overlap.

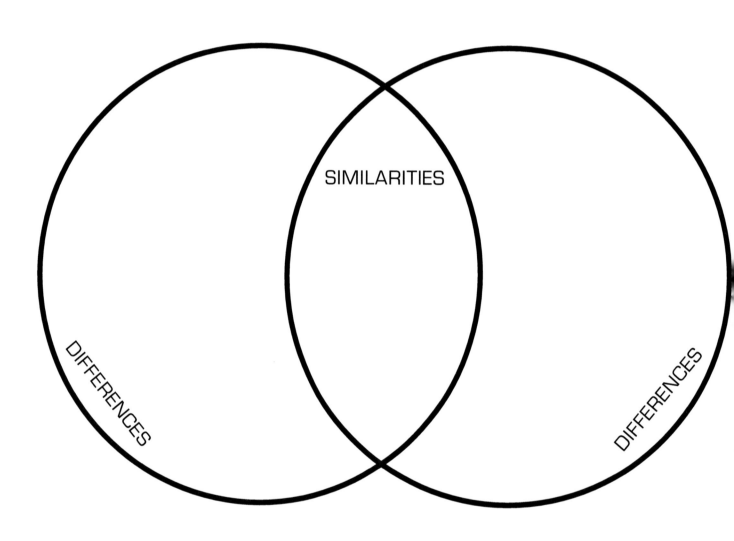

SIMILARITIES

DIFFERENCES

DIFFERENCES

Name _____ Date _____

TIMELINE

DATE

EVENT
Draw lines to connect the event to the correct year on the timeline.

SEQUENCE OF EVENTS CHART

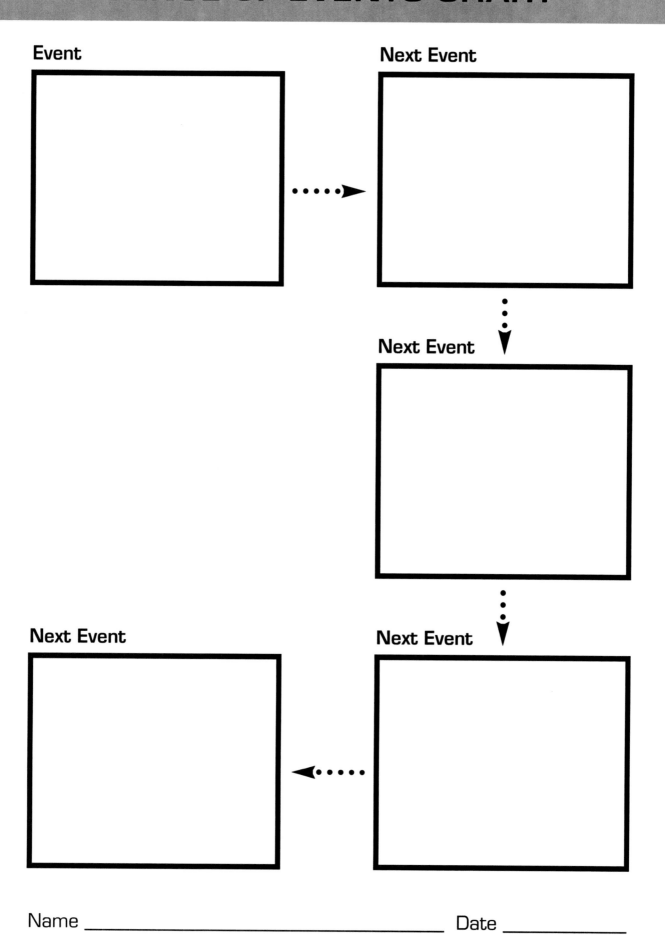

Event

Next Event

Next Event

Next Event

Next Event

Name _____ Date _____

T-CHART

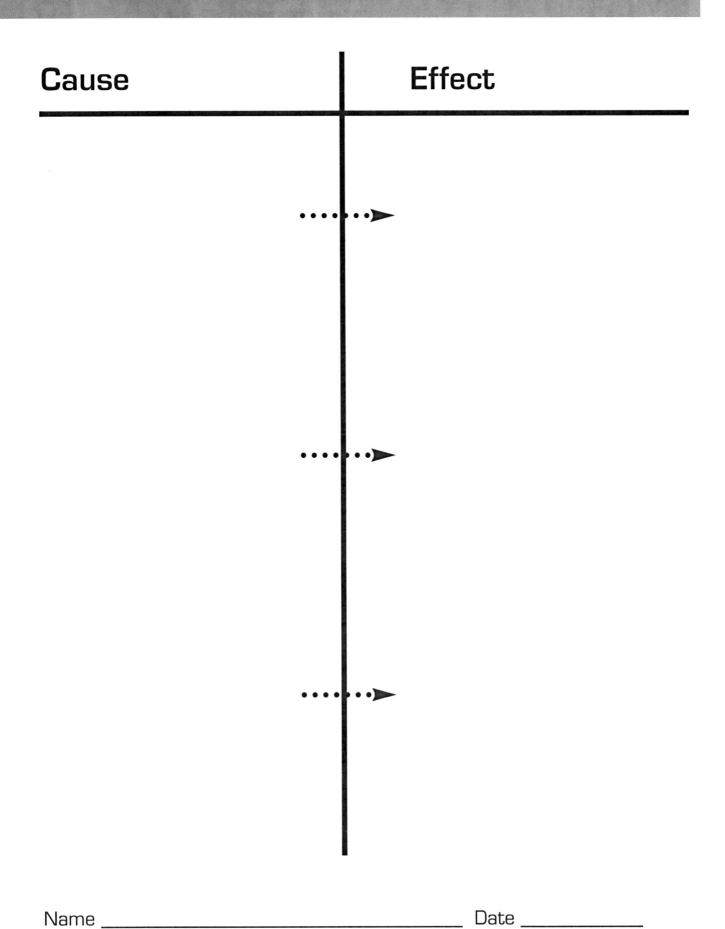

Cause	Effect

Name _____ Date _____

TEACHING GUIDE ANSWER KEY

CHECK-UP 1

1. (a) Zenger: a newspaper publisher accused of libel; Hamilton: most famous lawyer in the colonies; Hamilton successfully defended Zenger. (b) Washington: a Virginia militia officer; Braddock: a British general; Washington fought alongside Braddock and learned important lessons of war. (c) Johnson: a colonial with close ties to the Native Americans; Amherst: a British general; clashed over how to deal with Native Americans after the war. **2.** (a) first battle of French and Indian War (b) failure of alliance and union weakened colonial power. (c) British victory changed balance of power in North America. **3.** (a) publishing something unfavorable about someone; Zenger trial set precedents for colonial rights. (b) union of six Native American tribes; gave tribes negotiating power and inspired Franklin to suggest colonial union. (c) meeting to try to get Iroquois as British allies; failure made it harder for British to achieve victory. (d) Spanish settlements, each built around a church and a fort; Spanish built missions in California and the Southwest. **4.** Franklin believed the colonists should unite to strengthen themselves. **5.** Accept any well-reasoned analysis and opinion. **6.** Summaries should include French/British tensions, the American loss at Fort Duquesne, getting Native Americans to fight on the British side, the British and Native American victory at Lake George, British victories at Louisbourg and Quebec, and driving the French out of Canada and the land west of the Appalachians. **7.** (a) France lost its colonial claims in North America and French people in Canada came under the rule of Britain. (b) Spain temporarily gained Louisiana from France and temporarily lost Florida to Britain. (c) Native Americans gained nothing, and their land continued to be taken from them. **8.** Responses will vary. **9.** Responses will vary. **10.** *Conflicts:* colonists' identity as Americans, armed conflict of war, conflicts with Native Americans. *Changes:* colonists' feelings as Americans; balance of power with Britain, France, Native Americans.

CHECK-UP 2

1. (a) a colonial with close ties to the Native Americans, who negotiated treaty to allow settlers to move west of the Appalachians. (b) a frontiersman who led settlers west of the Appalachians. (c) a Frenchman who settled in the colonies and described Americans and American society. (d) an accomplished plantation manager who began South Carolina's indigo trade. **2.** (a) First a barrier to settlement; then colonists defied England by moving west of them, where they felt separated from British control. (b) Easy route for pioneers moving west, where they forged independent new lives. (c) Cut in the Appalachians that allowed pioneers to move west, where they felt more independent. **3.** (a) Religious movement that contributed to feelings of independence and change. (b) An English ban on settlement west of the Appalachians that colonists refused to obey. (c) A settler heading into new lands, strengthening ideas of independence. (d) Someone who owned and farmed own land, who gave the colonies a non-aristocratic tone. (e) A plant yielding a blue dye, which became a valuable commercial crop. (f) An English right to one's person that colonists expected to have. **4.** Crevecoeur believed Americans differed because they held new principles, thoughts, and opinions, which made them tolerant, independent, self-confident, free in thought, rich in opportunity, and able to think for themselves. **5.** Notes should include references to Pinckney's education, business ability, experimental nature, drive to keep learning new skills, and dedication to work. **6.** (a) Provided a foundation for individual rights. (b) Gave British people a Bill of Rights. **7.** Responses will vary. **8.** *Changes:* Movement west, where distance and challenges created greater sense of independence; new opportunities and diversity offered to Europeans; sense of independence as new challenges were met. *Conflict:* The more independent the colonists felt, the less happy they would be with English restrictions.

CHECK-UP 3

1. (a) The king of England and two of his important ministers wanted to bring the American colonists under tighter English control: George III and Townshend levied higher taxes on colonists, and Lord North ordered Boston harbor closed to shipping. (b) All three were firebrands of the American Revolution: Adams created trouble with the British, Paine wrote *Common Sense* to further the cause, and Henry gave fiery speeches advocating it. (c) All played a role in the Boston Massacre: Preston was the English officer in charge, Revere made a popular etching of the scene, Attucks was killed there, John Adams defended the English soldiers. (d) All played a role in the battles of Lexington and Concord: Revere, Dawes, and Prescott rode out to warn the colonists, and Parker commanded the minutemen. (e) They fought together at Fort Ticonderoga; Allen led the Green Mountain Boys, and Arnold fought there as a colonel in the Continental army. (f) All were Enlightenment thinkers: Newton was an English scientist, Locke was an English writer concerned with natural rights, and Rousseau was a French philosopher. **2.** (a) Colonists dumped British tea into Boston Harbor. (b) English troops fired on American colonists. (c) English troops tried to capture colonial munitions; minutemen fought back against them. **3.** (a) The parliament of the Iroquois nations, which impressed some colonists as a workable form of union. (b) Groups of prominent citizens who circulated letters among the colonies, helping colonists to communicate and solve problems. (c) An American army that gave Americans the chance to fight the British. (d) British law forcing colonists to house British soldiers, which angered colonists still more. (e) A meeting of delegates from the colonies who discussed mutual problems. **4.** Since the colonists were not represented in the English Parliament, the English had no right to tax them. England placed taxes on a variety of goods sold in America and that made Americans angry with English rule. **5.** Transportation and communication over land was on terrible roads that might be blocked by mud after storms or by miserable road conditions. The only other means was by boat, which was often slow. **6.** Possible responses: a British soldier might believe his life was threatened, a colonist might believe that British soldiers should not be in Boston anyway, and John Adams might believe that everyone has a right to a fair trial. **7.** British troops leave Boston to march to Concord, Revere learns they are taking the water route, Revere and others ride out to warn colonists, a small minutemen force assembles to resist the British, a shot rings out, and the two sides fight each other. **8.** *Changes:* colonist began to feel more like independent Americans and less like loyal British citizens; England changed its attitude about colonial financial responsibilities. *Conflict:* American resistance became stronger until finally there was armed conflict.

CHECK-UP 4

1. (a) Accepted Congress's offer of command of the Continental army. (b) Wrote the Declaration of Independence. (c) Became President of the Second Continental Congress. (d) Nominated Washington as commander of the army, served on the committee to write the Declaration of Independence, and did more than anyone to get the Declaration signed. (e) Served on the committee to write the Declaration. **2.** Responses will vary. **3.** (a) Separated Boston from Charlestown, where American forces had dug fortifications. (b) A town on the Charlestown peninsula where American forces stationed themselves. (c) A hill above Charlestown that American forces tried to defend against British attack. **4.** (a) British ships tried to sail into it to attack the South Carolina city of Charleston, but they failed. (b) Location of an unfinished fort in Charleston Harbor that the British failed to capture. (c) Sandbars in Charleston Harbor that British ships ran aground on. (d) Trees used for the walls of the that absorbed British cannonfire and made it useless. **5.** (a) A group of armed citizen soldiers; Washington had to make an army out of these untrained citizens. (b) A group of delegates meeting to discuss issues; by meeting, colonial leaders could take action and solve problems. (c) A statement colonists sent to Britain; their last attempt to solve problems with Britain peacefully. (d) A nickname for a signature; it is named for Hancock's bold signature on the Declaration of Independence. (e) Rule agreed to by those being ruled; it is the entire reason for having government, as stated in the Declaration. **6.** An army was being created, and George Washington was named its general; after Lexington and Concord, it seemed that war with the British was inevitable. **7.** These battles showed the colonists that they could stand up to the British and might even succeed in beating them. **8.** (a) The colonies must separate from Britain. (b) The king was abusing the rights of the colonists. (c) All men are created equal. (d) Citizens are entitled to certain rights that their government must not abuse. (e) Government must have the consent of the people it rules.

CHECK-UP 5

1. Conversations between each pair will vary. (a) Pitcher: colonial woman who brought water to soldiers during a battle; Brant: Mohawk widow of Sir William Johnson who fought for Great Britain. (b) Washington: wife of George Washington, who joined her husband at the front; Adams: wife of John Adams, who urged her husband to support equality for women. (c) Lafayette: French military officer who fought with the Americans; Steuben: German military officer who trained the American army. (d) Burgoyne: general who commanded British troops at Saratoga; Gates: general who commanded American troops at Saratoga. (e) Washington: commanded the Continental army; Clark: commanded American troops in battles in the West. 2. (a)Port city occupied by British during Revolutionary War. (b) Site of American victory over Hessian soldiers fighting on British side. (c) Site of American victory that was turning point in the war. (d) American army quarters during 1777-1778 winter. (e) Site of battles fought west of the Appalachians. 3. Responses should use the phrases noted to explain that the American forces were not professionals, that citizens of all kinds took an active role in the conflict, and that a spirit of unity and purpose in the army grew out of the terrible winter at Valley Forge. 4. (a) Forten supported the colonists because he too wanted equality. (b) He served as a powder boy aboard a ship and was captured by the British. (c) He wanted to retain his status as a free black in America. 5. Lafayette offered military help while Haym Salomon offered financial help. 6. Responses will vary. 7. Washington suffered along with his men, he kept their respect and loyalty, he often got them out of danger, and he helped them to develop the skills and spirit to go on fighting. 8. As a result of the Battle of Saratoga, the French came into the war on the American side, with supplies and military might. Americans probably felt proud after Bunker Hill because they stood up to the mighty British army, and somewhat hopeful that they could win. After Saratoga, they were probably much more proud, since an entire British army had surrendered, and with the French entry into the war, they could look forward to ultimate victory.

CHECK-UP 6

1. (a) Cornwallis: general commanding British troops at Yorktown; Clinton: commander in chief of British forces in America; Clinton was Cornwallis's boss. (b) De Grasse: commander of French fleet that prevented British fleet from relieving British forces at Yorktown. (c) Rochambeau and Washington: French general and American general who joined forces to cut off and defeat British at Yorktown. (d) Lafayette, Steuben, and Wayne: military leaders who joined Rochambeau and Washington at Yorktown. (e) Hamilton: American colonel who captured a key British fort at Yorktown. 2. (a) Spanish were founding settlements here. (b) These states were carved out of the Northwest Territory. 3. (a) Dividing the power to govern into three branches that balanced each other and kept each other in check. (b) Keeping government from forcing people to practice a certain religion. 4. Goddard printed the Declaration of Independence for circulation, she kept sources for articles she printed a secret to protect their authors, she took over jobs that were traditionally men's jobs, and she freed her slave and made her slave her heir. 5. (a) The Articles gave small and large states the same voting power. (b) The Articles did not prevent states from taxing one another, and they gave Congress no power to collect taxes to run the government. (c) The Articles did not provide for the organization of national military services or for their support. (d) Under the Articles, citizens felt more loyalty to their states than to a nation. 6. (a) Confederation Congress; (b) to provide for the eventual admission of states made from the Northwest Territory; (c) west of the Appalachians and north of the Ohio River, originally claimed by Britain; (d) Ohio, Illinois, Indiana, Michigan, Wisconsin, and part of Minnesota; (e) freedom of religion, *habeas corpus*, trial by jury, no slavery, establishment of public schools 7. Responses will vary. 8. Once the common enemy had been defeated, the 13 states found that they had conflicting means of dealing with their problems and were acting more like separate and competing states rather than a unified nation.

CHECK-UP 7

1. Summaries might include Madison's role in organizing the Constitutional Convention, the knowledge of government he brought with him, the Virginia Plan he wrote, his note-taking, and the Bill of Rights he wrote. 2. Responses will vary. 3. (a) A government made up of a group of partners; it was favored by Framers who did not want a strong central government. (b) A government that divides power between a central government and state governments; it was favored by Framers who wanted a strong central government. (c) A lawmaking body; part of the separation of powers. (d) The government's leader— a President or king; part of the separation of powers. (e) The court system; part of the separation of powers. (f) Divisions of the legislature. (g) An addition to the Constitution; allowed the Constitution to be changed. (h) To approve; the states had to approve the Constitution before it could become the law of the land. 4. Responses will vary, but should include explanation of human rights and freedom, self-government through representatives, and each branch of government limiting the others. 5. The Virginia Plan said representation in Congress should be based on population, the New Jersey Plan said all states should have the same number of representatives, and the Connecticut Compromise said all states should have equal representation (two) in the Senate and a number of representatives in the House based on population. 6. Responses will vary but might include the oppressive and unfair nature of slavery, the perceived economic need for it, and the need to get all the states to accept the Constitution. 7. Mason believed that the Constitution was not good enough and that it should have outlawed slavery. Henry wanted powerful states, not a federal republic. Madison argued that the Constitution would protect individual rights. Franklin argued that it was better than nothing. 8. The major conflicts in changing the form of government concerned power: the division of power between a strong central government and the states, the division of power between large and small states. Students may also include decisions about the structure of the federal government and the unresolved conflicts over slavery.

RESOURCE PAGE 1

1. 1750 map: British—13 colonies British; French—all of the territory west of the Appalachians and Canada; Spanish—Florida. 2. 1763 map: British—13 colonies, territory west of the Appalachians to the Mississippi, and Canada; Spanish—Florida and territory west of the Mississippi.

RESOURCE PAGE 2

Students should respond with such specifics as natural beauty and variety, which hints at fertile soil for farming, as do ample plains. Water is also present in abundance, as the Ohio River and the sweetwater spring show. And the hunting is good, which makes for a bountiful food supply.

RESOURCE PAGE 3

1. Approximately 1,300 miles. 2. Massachusetts, Connecticut, New York, New Jersey, Pennsylvania, Delaware, Maryland, Virginia, North Carolina, South Carolina. 3. About 5 days. 4. About 52 days

RESOURCE PAGE 4

A. From top to bottom, order of colonies should be Virginia, Massachusetts, Pennsylvania, Maryland, North Carolina, Connecticut, New York, South Carolina, New Jersey, New Hampshire, Rhode Island, Delaware, Georgia. Each should have appropriate bar length. B. Students' riddles will vary.

RESOURCE PAGE 5

1. Students' maps should have a blue line along the crest of Breed's Hill and a red arrow stretching from Boston to Charlestown and up to Breed's Hill. 2. The British also bombarded the American lines with cannons. 3. Students' maps should have a dotted red line leading, either by land or over water, from Boston and going around the Charlestown peninsula to the neck of land at the north end of the peninsula. Speculations should center around British belief that the Americans would not put up a battle when confronted with British troops.

RESOURCE PAGE 6

1. 7.3 percent. 2. 10,623. 3. 5.3 percent. 4. $436.36. 5. Responses will vary, but should include that the costs of the war were overwhelming, and since Congress could not raise money by taxation, it had to borrow from people like Haym Salomon.

RESOURCE PAGE 7

1. York River, James River, Chesapeake Bay. **2.** The British navy could supply and protect his troops from the sea. **3.** Using the estimate in the textbook of 500 miles between White Plains and Yorktown, the army traveled approximately 12.5 miles a day. **4.** The French navy, under Comte de Grasse, had defeated the British navy, under Admiral Graves, at Chesapeake Bay, and so the British navy could not bring supplies or reinforcements to Cornwallis, or help him retreat.

RESOURCE PAGE 8

1. Congress now had the sole right to pass the laws the nation needed. **2.** The states will make the rules for electing their representatives, so that elections will be held regularly. **3.** The United States will establish a judicial system, whose powers will be exercised by the Supreme Court and other courts Congress will establish. **4.** The President of the United States, who holds civil power, will be Commander in Chief of the military services, and thus military power is not superior to civil power.

RESOURCE PAGE 9

Part I: 1. I, 2; **2.** I, 3; **3.** I, 8; **4.** II, 1; **5.** II, 2; **6.** III, 2; **7.** IV, 3; **8.** V, 9; **9.** VI; **10.** VII. **Part II: 1.** I; **2.** I; **3.** VII; **4.** III; **5.** VI. Students should include specific references to the Constitution in describing the separation of powers, the system of checks and balances, and the Bill of Rights.

STUDENT STUDY GUIDE ANSWER KEY

Answers for writing prompts and open-ended activities are not included in this key.

CHAPTER 1

Word Bank 1. arbitrary **2.** indentured servant **3.** disbarred **4.** apprentice **5.** libel.
Making Inferences 1. AG **2.** AG **3.** D **4.** D **5.** AG **6.** D.

CHAPTER 2

Fact or Opinion 1. O **2.** F **3.** F **4.** F **5.** O.
Primary Sources 1. pay 15,000 pounds of tobacco **2.** $75, **3.** $11, 250 **4.** due on Christmas.

CHAPTER 3

Word Bank 1. musket **2.** frontier **3.** surveyor
Sequence of Events 3, 1, 5, 4, 2.
Primary Sources 1. French and Indians **2.** French and Indians **3.** Discuss students' answers.

CHAPTER 4

Word Bank 1. baronet **2.** sachem **3.** feudal lord.
Drawing Conclusions 1. a, b **2.** a, c **3.** a, c.
Primary Sources 1. good, personality **2.** calm **3.** friendly **4.** Ask students to read work aloud

CHAPTER 5

Word Bank 1. foreign secretary **2.** diplomat.
Map 1. a **2.** c **3.** c **4.** a.
Primary Sources 1. fifty yards **2.** waited until they were twenty yards **3.** 15 minutes **4.** Braddock at Fort Duquesne

CHAPTER 6

Word Bank 1. mission **2.** presidio
Primary Source 1. kill **2.** execute **3.** elimination **4.** Ask students to read euphemisms aloud.

CHAPTER 7

Word Bank roots: awake, proclaim, speculate.
Map 1. c **2.** b **3.** a **4.** Ask students to read answers aloud.
Primary Source 1. left family **2.** home **3.** west **4.** to find Kentucky.

CHAPTER 8

Fact or Opinion 1. F **2.** O **3.** O **4.** F **5.** O **6.** F.

CHAPTER 9

Word Bank 1. Her sons would play important roles in the trouble that was brewing with England. **2.** Indigo was a valuable blue dye much desired in Europe.
Drawing Conclusions 1. a, c **2.** a, c **3.** b, c.
Primary Source 1. I am in charge of three plantations. **2.** business letters. Discuss other answers. **3.** discuss.

CHAPTER 10

Sequence of Events 1. B **2.** A **3.** B **4.** B **5.** B **6.** B **7.** A **8.** A.
Primary Sources 1. "ancient" in first line **2.** power **3.** does not like him.

CHAPTER 11

Primary Sources Have students read headlines and new stories aloud. Discuss.
Writing Have students display and explain commemorative stamps. Vote for best representations.

CHAPTER 12

Word Bank 1. deist **2.** firebrand **3.** committee of correspondence.
Drawing Conclusions 1. P **2.** H **3.** H **4.** A **5.** A **6.** P **7.** H **8.** P.
Primary Sources 1. dislike **2.** United States.

CHAPTER 13

Word Bank 1. Quartering Act, redcoats **2.** Continental Congress **3.** deserters **4.** Boston Massacre. Ask students to read sentences aloud.
Sequence of Events 7, 3, 1, 5, 2, 8, 4, 6.
Primary Sources 1. jury **2.** convict soldiers of murder **3.** facts don't always agree with one's emotions.

CHAPTER 14

Word Bank 1. patriot, minuteman, Loyalist.
Making Inferences 1. P **2.** B **3.** P **4.** P **5.** P **6.** B **7.** P **8.** B.
Primary Sources 1. killed **2.** brave (discuss).

CHAPTER 15

Word Bank Green Mountain Boys: **1.** comprised of Ethan Allen and friends **2.** They boasted of prowess with rifles **3.** Tried to force New Yorkers from New Hampshire. Enlightenment: **1.** spurred by Newton **2.** time of widespread intellectual experimentation **3.** world could be understood with study and observation.
Map 1. Connecticut River **2.** Hartford **3.** the Connecticut River separates New Hampshire and Vermont.
Primary Sources 1. great desire (discuss other answers) **2.** Indians or Native Americans **3.** people who move to the frontier **4.** have drunk.

CHAPTER 16

Word Bank 1. legislative authority **2.** commonwealth.
Fact or Opinion 1. F **2.** O **3.** F **4.** O **5.** F **6.** O.
Primary Source 1. his face **2.** determination **3.** spirit is energy **4.** wit comes from a person; humor is appreciation of another's wit.

CHAPTER 17

Word Bank 1. The Continental Congress tried to patch things up with England. **2.** An olive branch is a symbol of peace. **3.** The colonists asked the King to consider their problems.
Main Idea 1. a, b **2.** a, c **3.** b, c.
Primary Sources 1. disagreements or objections **2.** defeat, punishment, death **3.** allowing colonists to govern themselves **4.** England.

CHAPTER 18

Word Bank 1. earthworks **2.** bayonets **3.** barracks, fortifications.
Sequence of Events 7, 1, 2, 4, 3, 5, 6.
Primary Sources 1. dislikes him **2.** "happily killed" **3.** patriots **4.** discuss.

CHAPTER 19

Map 1. Georgia **2.** warm, humid. **3.** Sullivan Island is on the Atlantic in a hot climate and palm trees grow there naturally.
Drawing Conclusions 1. a, c **2.** a, b **3.** a, c.
Primary Source 1. Parliament **2.** Sullivan's Island **3.** Yankee.

CHAPTER 20 / CHAPTER 21
Words in Context 1. b 2. a 3. c 4. b 5. a.
Primary Sources 1. universal father 2. emotions 3. senses 4. we are all equal.

CHAPTER 22
Word Bank 1. hardtack 2. blockade.
Fact or Opinion 1. F 2. F 3. O 4. O 5. O 6. F 7. O 8. F 9. O.
Primary Sources 1. Revolution is taking place 2. care 3. won't obey 4. no vote

CHAPTER 23
Word Bank 1. powder boy, privateer. 2. pueblo.
Sequence of Events 1. A 2. B 3. B, 4. A 5. B 6. A 7. A 8. B.
Primary Sources 1. allow them to die 2. soldiers 3. Discuss.

CHAPTER 24 / CHAPTER 25
Word Bank 1. marquis 2. drillmaster, recruits, regulars 3. dragoon.
Sequence of Events 1. A 2. B 3. B 4. A 5. B 6. A 7. A 8. B.
Drawing Conclusions 1. c 2. c 3. b.
Primary Sources 1. defender of Liberty 2. interesting republic 3.-4. Discuss

CHAPTER 26
Word Bank 1. retreat. 2.Hessians 3. mercenaries. pueblo.
Main Idea 1.a 2. a 3.c.
Primary Sources 1. lack 2. earthworks 3. preparation 4. Have students read re-statements aloud

CHAPTER 27
Word Bank 1. oath of allegiance 2. guerilla 3. sniper.
Cause and Effect 1.b 2. c 3. e 4. a.
Map 1.c 2. c 3. a 4. b.

CHAPTER 28
Map 1. ~650 miles. 2. Ohio river, Mississippi river, Great Lakes
Word Bank 1. quartermaster 2. mutiny 3. serfs.
Primary Sources 1. poor living conditions 2. ragged clothes, rotten food 3. drafty fireplaces. 4. Read answers aloud.

CHAPTER 29
Word Bank 1. legislative branch 2. constitution 3. judicial branch 4. executive branch
Making Inferences 1. b 2. c 3. b 4. a 5. c.
Primary Sources 1. early civilization 2. people 3. discussing, thinking 4. democracy.

CHAPTER 30
Word Bank satire, irony, irony.
Fact or Opinion 1.O 2. F 3. F 4.O 5. F 6.O 7. F 8. F.
Primary Sources 1. president 2. give orders 3.women are equal.

CHAPTER 31
Sequence of Events 1. A 2. B 3. B 4. A 5. B 6. A 7. B 8. A.
Primary Sources 1. Yorktown. 2. Change in people attitudes about monarchy. 3. A war is one part of a revolution, which is greater and farther reaching. 4. sweeping change

CHAPTER 32
Word Bank 1. Articles of Confederation 2. supply and demand 3. inflation.
Drawing Conclusions 1. c 2. b 3. a.
Map 1. Virginia 2. New Hampshire, Rhode Island, New Jersey, Delaware, Maryland, South Carolina, 3. Connecticut, 4.Virginia, New York, North Carolina, Georgia.

CHAPTER 33
Word Bank 1. involuntary servitude 2. ordinance, townships 3. Conestoga.
Main Idea 1. c 2. b 3. b.

CHAPTER 34
Word Bank 1. piedmont 2. separation of church and state 3. decimal, intellectual.
Making Inferences 1. G 2. A 3. F 4. R 5. R 6. R 7. R 8. G.
Primary Sources 1.United States 2. we are proud 3. religious beliefs.

CHAPTER 35 / CHAPTER 36
Word Bank 1.Virginia Plan 2. Constitutional Convention 3. median 4. Framers.
Sequence of Events 1. O 2. F 3. O 4. F 5. F 6. O 7. O 8. F.
Primary Sources 1. agreeable, eloquent 2. soft-spoken 3. good vocabulary 4. win votes.

CHAPTER 37
Word Bank 1. federation 2. federal 3. confederation 4. federalism.
Making Inferences 1. F 2. F 3. C 4. C 5. F.
Primary Sources 1. sun. 2. planets. 3. prefer the relatively equal pull of the other planets to the centralizing pull of the sun. 4. prefer the strong central pull of the sun to the weaker pull of the planets.

CHAPTER 38 / CHAPTER 39
Word Bank 1.Virginia Plan, New Jersey Plan 2. Connecticut Plan, Great Compromise 3. Three Fifths Compromise 4. checks and balances, supreme law 5. amendment 6. ratify.
Primary Sources 1. little influence 2. people don't have information 3. No. Discuss.

CHAPTER 40
Word Bank 1. Preamble 2. slave trade 3. cotton gin.
Main Idea 1. c 2. b 3. b.

CHAPTER 41
Making Inferences 1. D 2. D 3. R 4. D 5. R 6. D 7. R 8. R.
Primary Sources 1. delegates 2. meeting of officials 3. document or constitution 4. disagree.

CHAPTER 42
Word Bank 1. republic 2. Bill of Rights 3. Anti-Federalist.
Fact or Opinion 1. F 2. O 3. F 4. O 5. O 6. O 7. F.
Primary Sources 1. divine Providence 2. rebellions was punished by death 3. could lose homes 4. deep beliefs.

Printed in the United States
124905LV00001B/67-68/P